THE BEATLES

All you ever wanted to know about the Fab Four

igloobooks

Published in 2017
by Igloo Books Ltd
Cottage Farm
Sywell
NN6 0BJ
www.igloobooks.com

HUN001 1117
2 4 6 8 10 9 7 5 3
ISBN 978-1-78557-705-5

Cover image: © CBW / Alamy Stock Photo
Back cover images: © iStock / Getty Images

Cover designed by Nicholas Gage
Edited by Natalie Baker

Written by Kim Aitken

Printed and manufactured in China

Contents

Introduction

Four men from Liverpool, England, each with a gift for music, came together in 1960 to create the most commercially successful and critically acclaimed rock act of all time.

John Lennon, Paul McCartney, George Harrison, and Ringo Starr would become famous together as the 'Fab Four'.

The Beatles had a magical chemistry, built on a singer-songwriter coupling between Lennon and McCartney, which was to become to many a musical marriage made in heaven. Theirs was a winning formula that would lead to more Number One albums on the British charts and the highest selling singles in the UK.

Inspired by the rock and roll breakthrough led by Elvis Presley, as well as skiffle, a jazz, blues, and folk blend, the group performed a variety of types of hits, from pop rock and ballads to psychedelic rock.

Hitting the scene in the early 60s with their creative style and sing-along songs, their massive fan base grew to be described as 'Beatlemania'. But this was not born of overnight success; the band had gained a following after playing venue after venue in Liverpool and Hamburg, Germany over a long three-year period.

Left to right; Paul McCartney, George Harrison, John Lennon, and Ringo Starr of the Beatles, taking a dip in a swimming pool while on tour in the USA

The Beatles playing live in 1963

Love Me Do was a modest success in the UK in 1962, but it kick started international stardom for the group, leading what was dubbed the 'British Invasion' in the United States of America. Halfway into their ten-year reign as the rock group of the swinging sixties, The Beatles recorded innovative and progressive hits unique to them.

In four years, The Beatles cut six albums that were and still are widely regarded as those that defined the rock era, and remain hugely influential with musicians and singers.

At the time, the media and fan-base described a 'fifth Beatle' – Brian Epstein – the band's manager who helped shaped the band into a slick live performance act.

The fascination with the group's recording success also meant a fascination with the band members' private lives and antics. As a group of young men exposed to the trappings of fame and fortune, they enjoyed the 60s lifestyle, which for rock stars meant girls, drugs, and parties. The Beatles' wives later also became a source of interest for the media and the general public.

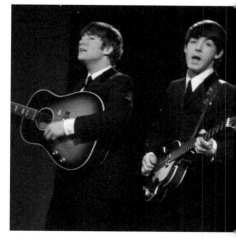

John Lennon (left) and Paul McCartney play on the set of a TV show in 1964

The Beatles pose for an early group portrait wearing Pierre Cardin collarless jackets

The Beatles pose for a magazine spread in 1964

After the band broke up in 1970, each of The Beatles enjoyed successful solo careers in varying degrees. Sadly, Lennon died in 1980, after being shot in the street by a mentally disturbed fan. In 2001, Harrison passed away from lung cancer. The last two Beatles, McCartney and Starr are, more than 50 years later, both active in the music industry and still perform live shows.

In addition to the success the band had in the UK, The Beatles are the best-selling band in the US, with sales of 177 million singles and albums (according to the Recording Industry Association of America).

Their record for the most number one hits on the Hot 100 chart, with 20 singles, was still in place at the time of print.

With 19 albums in the US and 15 in the UK, The Beatles still hold more Number One records than any other group. They spent the highest number of weeks at Number One in the albums chart in both countries.

They also hold the most successful first week of sales for a double album, The Beatles Anthology Volume 1, which was released 25 years after the band broke up. They are still the best-selling musical group of all time – record label EMI estimates they have sold over one billion discs and tapes worldwide.

"The Beatles will go on and on."

- George Harrison

The fab four wave to fans on July 2nd, 1964 as they return to London from a tour of Australia

Lennon and McCartney in 1963

THE BEGINNING:
Lennon and McCartney

John Lennon was still in school, aged 16, when he formed a skiffle (a jazz-blues-folk blend) group, The Quarrymen. Named after the school the friends attended, Quarry Bank in Liverpool, the band was led by singer Lennon. It was 1957.

Playing at a fete for the St. Peter's Church in Woolton, Liverpool, the band was setting up their equipment when the bass player, Ivan Vaughan, introduced Paul McCartney, who he'd met at the Liverpool Institute. McCartney, himself just 15, showed Lennon how to tune a guitar.

"I remember coming into the fete and seeing all the sideshows. And also hearing all this great music wafting in from this little Tannoy system. It was John and the band.

"I remember I was amazed and thought, 'Oh great', because I was obviously into the music. I remember John singing a song called Come Go With Me. He'd heard it on the radio. He didn't really know the verses, but he knew the chorus. The rest he just made up himself.

"I just thought, 'Well, he looks good, he's singing well and he seems like a great lead singer to me.' Of course, he had his glasses off, so he really looked suave. I remember John was good. He was really the only outstanding member, all the rest kind of slipped away."
– *Paul McCartney, 1995, interview with Record Collector magazine*

John Lennon in school uniform in 1948

After demonstrating his singing and musical abilities, which Lennon immediately admired and was intimidated by, McCartney was offered a place in the band. McCartney took some time to decide on joining, but eventually became their rhythm guitarist.

Later, George Harrison, who knew McCartney from the bus ride into the Liverpool Institute, was invited to watch them play. Harrison, then 14 years old, was initially deemed by Lennon to be too young to join.

Keen to convince Lennon that Harrison was not too young, McCartney had helped to organize and stage a second audition for Harrison, held on the top deck of a Liverpool bus, and Harrison played 'raunchy' guitar for Lennon. But after playing for Lennon – wowing him – and pestering him for a month to join,

Harrison was their new lead guitarist.

A year later, Lennon's friends from the Quarry Bank had departed. Then, while attending the Liverpool College of Art, Lennon met Stuart Sutcliffe, who was first and foremost an artist. The sale of one of his pieces meant he could buy a new bass guitar and he ended up joining as bassist in 1960. Interestingly, it was Sutcliffe's suggestion that they call themselves The Beatles in honor of Buddy Holly and the Crickets. They used the name the Silver Beatles until August of 1960.

By September 1960, they had formed and renamed the band The Beatles, although at this point they still had Sutcliffe on bass and a man named Pete Best on drums. They had not yet met Ringo Starr.

The Quarrymen perform onstage at their first concert at the Casbah Coffee House

The Beatles before Ringo

Before the band was formed in its entirety, the legendary writing partnership between Lennon and McCartney was developing. While the two were very adept at creating song lyrics of a very high standard on their own, and did so often, they were at their best together.

The boys, then only aged 15, shared musical interests and influences. They were obsessed with Elvis Presley.

"Nothing really affected me until I heard Elvis. If there hadn't been Elvis, there would not have been The Beatles."

– *John Lennon*

Lennon and McCartney also loved to imitate the sound of Buddy Holly, the Everley Brothers, and Smokey Robinson & the Miracles. They also shared with each other the sounds of musical talents Carl Perkins, Chuck Berry, Little Richard, Eddie Cochran, and Roy Orbison.

Shaping their songwriting partnership at McCartney's family home in Liverpool, the Liverpool Institute, and at Lennon's Aunt Mimi's house, they would perform their newly written songs to friends, including George Harrison, Nigel Walley, Barbara Baker, and Lennon's art school colleagues.

McCartney said of Aunt Mimi, "[she] was very aware that John's friends were lower class," claiming she would patronize him. At the same time, McCartney's father was said to be unhappy about his son's friendship with Lennon, as McCartney's brother Mike said his father thought Lennon would "get him into trouble."

The Beatles perform on stage at the Cavern Club in February 1961, Pete Best is on drums

A poster for The Beatles Show at The Rialto Ballroom, Liverpool, September 6th, 1962

As they continued writing together in the 60s, Lennon and McCartney kept up this love of musical discovery – as the duo listened to Bob Dylan, Frank Zappa, and The Beach Boys they tapped into their inspiration with revolutionary new sounds. Indeed, the producer of The Beatles, George Martin said later of the breakthrough album Sergeant Pepper's Lonely Hearts Club Band, "Without Pet Sounds, Sgt. Pepper wouldn't have happened ...Pepper was an attempt to equal Pet Sounds."

As they were learning to complement each other's writing ability, they found a rhythm and approach Lennon called "writing eyeball-to-eyeball" and "playing into each other's noses," by which he meant one of the pair would outline lyrics or a verse and the other would complete it with a bridge section and supplement the lyrics.

In this process, they would develop a mutual respect for each other but also undercover a competitiveness between them. Regardless, their combination meant a good song was developed and shaped into a great one – any ideas or fragments became whole and nothing shy of genius.

For many, the combination of Lennon-McCartney was the main reason for the band's success and uniqueness.

Despite this spark and connection musically, they struggled to manage their relationship at times and, in particular, who would receive credit for the songwriting. Both gave interviews to Playboy magazine in the 80s, individually and separately, giving considerable insight into their perception of each other during this process:

Lennon told the magazine in 1980, "He provided a lightness, an optimism, while I would always go for the sadness, the discords, the bluesy notes. There was a period when I thought I didn't write melodies, that Paul wrote those and I just wrote straight, shouting rock 'n' roll. But, of course, when I think of some of my own songs – 'In My Life', or some of the early stuff, 'This Boy' – I was writing melody with the best of them."

When McCartney was interviewed by the same magazine four years later, he said of the song Help! "John and I wrote it at his house in Weybridge for the film." He said he helped Lennon with the 'countermelody' and weighted it 70-30 in ratio to Lennon. Largely recognized as a Lennon song, this comment from McCartney contradicted popular thought.

A vinyl LP for Sgt. Pepper's Lonely Hearts Club Band by The Beatles

John Lennon (left) and Paul McCartney, at the offices of Brian
Epstein's NEMS Enterprises Management Company

Other songs that have had conflicting accounts by the pair include Ticket to Ride, In My Life, and Eleanor Rigby. Lennon claimed 70 percent of the lyrics to Eleanor while his childhood friend, Pete Shotton, said Lennon's contribution to that song was "absolutely nil" and McCartney said he wrote it himself while playing piano.

Later, McCartney claimed in 1994 that the song Tell Me What You See was wholly his, while years earlier he had said it was only 60 percent written by him, the remainder being Lennon's contribution.

There was a significant difference between the two musicians' accounts of how they worked together and who wrote which song, or the majority of the lyrics. What seemed to be consistent, however, is that the composition and lyrics of a song were written by both artists – they did not have one role as composer and one role as lyricist, which was unlike most music writing partnerships.

Interestingly, especially considering all their conversations about who should be credited for various lyrics, they had, by accounts, agreed when they met around 15 years of age that before they had fully formed the band they would share the writing credits on an even and equal basis, regardless of whether one or both of them penned a song. Between them, they wrote and composed 180 songs credited as Lennon-McCartney, making up the majority of The Beatles' recorded tracks.

John Lennon (playing Fender Jazzmaster guitar) & Paul McCartney in session during the photo shoot for the 'Help' album cover in Obertauern

Paul McCartney waiting in Epstein's offices

The first recording (that is not The Beatles) released, labeled, and credited 'Lennon-McCartney' was You'll Be Mine in 1960, although the first tracks originally penned were believed to be much earlier in 1957, and reportedly primarily written by Lennon. They were Hello Little Girl and One After 909.

In the early years of the band's formation, some of the compositions were credited to McCartney and Harrison, as well as Lennon and Harrison. Come 1962, the join credit agreement was employed, with (only a few exceptions) almost all songs published from this year on released as 'Lennon-McCartney.'

Some examples of the dynamic duo's combined efforts included A Day in the Life, where the lyrics 'Woke up, fell out of bed, dragged a comb across my head' helped develop Lennon's 'I read the news today, oh boy.' Another famous song under this category was Hey Jude, where McCartney's worry over the lyrics 'the movement you need is on your shoulder,' was alleviated by Lennon's reassurance that it was the best in the song.

Lennon had said of their winning combination, in that same Playboy interview of 1980, that their purpose or intention was to communicate and that he and McCartney shared this belief. As their career progressed, more and more songs would be written by one of the pair.

In the first two albums released by The Beatles, however, only one track was written by someone other than the Lennon-McCartney partnership, that being Harrison's Don't Bother Me. In addition, the third album A Hard Day's Night featured only the pair's writing, followed by Beatles for Sale, which consisted of Lennon-McCartney numbers and covers.

John Lennon & Paul McCartney returning to
Heathrow Airport from vacation in Greece

23

The first single released by The Beatles in 1962, Love Me Do, was credited to 'Lennon–McCartney.' The following songs released, Please Please Me, From Me to You, were credited 'McCartney–Lennon.'

By 1963, the songwriting credits were back to 'Lennon–McCartney,' for the release of She Loves You. This order for the credits followed for all remaining Beatles singles co-written by them.

This ordering of the songwriters' names was highlighted again much later when McCartney released his 1976 album Wings over America, featuring the credits for five of The Beatles' songs as 'McCartney–Lennon.'

While Lennon was alive, there was no conversation about the ordering of the credits. However, after his death, McCartney and Lennon's widow, Yoko Ono had a disagreement over the order.

When Ono expressed an objection to the credit order for Yesterday, McCartney said Lennon had agreed either of them could reverse the order if they released any in the future. In the end, McCartney conceded and said, "I'm happy with the way it is and always has been. Lennon and McCartney is still the rock 'n' roll trademark I'm proud to be a part of – in the order it has always been."

Later, there would be a couple of Harrison and Starr-written songs (Starr's famously being Octopus's Garden), but for the large majority of Beatles recordings, their contribution was vital to the band's success.

In 1960, having formed and renamed the band The Beatles, at Sutcliffe's suggestion, they consisted of Lennon, McCartney, Sutcliffe, and Harrison, but lacked a permanent drummer. At their unofficial then-manager Allan Williams' request they held an audition and discovered Pete Best.

Top: The Beatles perform in Liverpool's Cavern Club, with Pete Best on drums, 1962

Above: Pete Best in 1960 – he was later fired and replaced with Ringo Starr

John Lennon playing and singing with Paul McCartney at Vigorelli Velodrome. Milan, June 1965

The Beatles onstage at the
London Palladium during
a performance in front of
2,000 screaming fans

From Liverpool to Hamburg

The Beatles, now a fully formed five-piece rock band, had secured a contract with a club in Hamburg, Germany for three-and-a-half months.

Contrary to the image presented of The Beatles when they first hit the charts in the UK and the US, in their early Liverpool-Hamburg days, the group wore rockabilly style hair, black leather jackets, and black leather trousers. They played in small, sweaty clubs night after night. They smoked and drank and dabbled in prescription drugs to get through the relentless late night performances.

In what grew into over two and a half years of residency, the band played 281 gigs, traveling five times between Liverpool and Hamburg. It was reported that in 1961, The Beatles played 98 nights in a row, without a break. Often, they were expected to start playing at 7pm and play for the next 12 hours solid.

The Beatles cut their teeth on these gigs, learning to improvise and expand their repertoire to cover the time they were performing.

Harrison described the Hamburg residency as an apprenticeship, and it was where they were to cut their first single, as the backing band for rock singer Tony Sheridan.

The main venue the band were residents of, owned by Bruno Koschmider, was called the Indra Club, described as a small, dingy venue that was also a strip tease joint and was located on the outskirts of the red light district of Hamburg, Reeperbahn. On the band's arrival, they immediately played the Indra Club, followed by a stint at the Kaiserkeller after the Indra had to be closed down following noise complaints.

Their accommodation was equally grimy, with a couple of storage rooms as bedrooms in the back of a cinema, "It was a pig sty," Lennon recalled. "We were right next to the ladies' toilet."

The Beatles performing during their first Hamburg trip

The Beatles pose for a photo shoot in a backyard, 1963

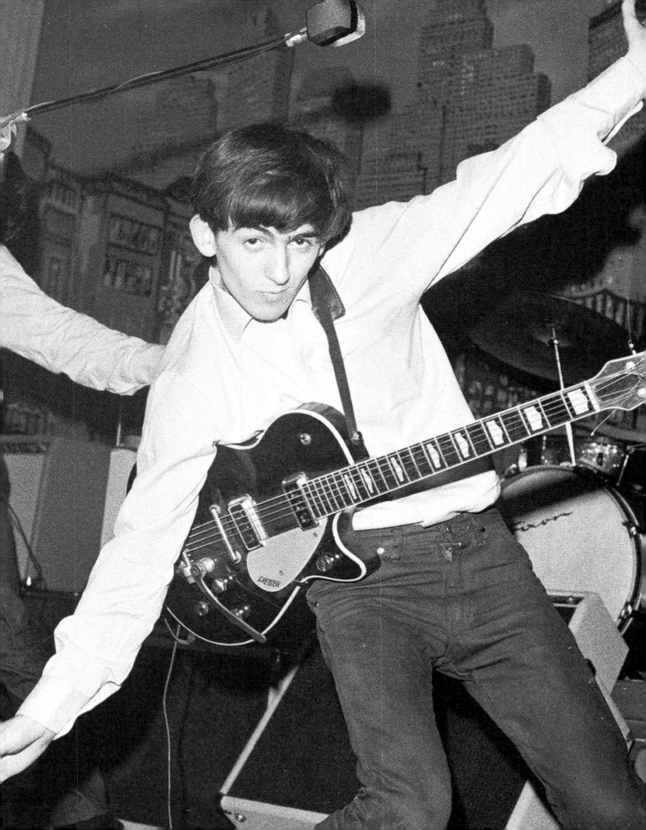

An interesting time for the band followed shortly afterwards. Contracted exclusively to Koschmider's clubs, the band upset him by playing at a rival club, called Top Ten. He ended their contract with one month's notice and sought revenge by reporting Harrison's being underage to the authorities. Harrison was deported, having lied on his visa application about his age. Just a week later, Koschmider reported McCartney and Best to the police for setting fire to a wall tapestry in their room. They were arrested for arson and were also deported from Germany.

Having established a rock and roll approach quite early in their career, the tone was set for The Beatles' rebellious behavior.

"We didn't all get into music for a job! We got into music to avoid a job, in truth – and get lots of girls."

"Hamburg totally wrecked us. I remember getting home to England and my dad thought I was half-dead. I looked like a skeleton, I hadn't noticed the change, I'd been having such a ball!"

– *Paul McCartney*

Naturally, the deportations separated the band members for a few months, especially as Sutcliffe had met and got engaged to a German girl, Astrid Kirchherr. She was the first person to photograph The Beatles as a band for promotional purposes, in a professional sense.

It was during this period that they experimented with drugs, music, and fashion. To begin with, the group tried the prescription 'upper' Preludin recreationally, and learned they could maintain their night-long performances.

Even their haircuts were experimental and existential. Sutcliffe's fiancée cut his hair into the style that would later be adopted by all band members.

John Lennon at The Star Club in Hamburg, 1962

George Harrison in Hamburg, 1962

In 1961 Sutcliffe left the band, and resumed his art studies in Germany.

In his absence and with some 'experimental' time on his hands, McCartney learned how to play bass guitar. They had become a four-piece.

Still only teenagers, the 'Fab Four' had little in the way of formal musical education, and yet they knew that would become something big. Harrison said, 'we just had this amazing inner feeling of: "We're going to do it'. I don't know why... we were just cocky." Lennon's Aunt Mimi continued to be mortified by Lennon's career direction and begged him to return to art studies. It was too late though for Lennon was hooked on music.

The producer Bert Kaempfert decided to contract the group through to June 1962, using them as a sometime backing band for Tony Sheridan's recordings.

Following their second residency in Hamburg, the group was gaining recognition and a following in Merseyside, dubbed the 'Merseybeat' movement.

In late 1961, when The Beatles played one of hundreds of gigs at Liverpool's Cavern Club, they met local record storeowner and music columnist Brian Epstein, who said, "I immediately liked what I heard. They were fresh and they were honest, and they had what I thought was a sort of presence ... [a] star quality."

Having no prior experience managing a band, Epstein was initially rejected by the group.

Top: Paul McCartney on stage at the Cavern nightclub in Liverpool

Above: The Cavern Club in Liverpool, where The Beatles had a residency in the early 1960s

Paul McCartney and John Lennon of The Beatles perform onstage at Ernst Merck Halle on their final German tour

Stuart Sutcliffe posed in a Hamburg street in April 1961

In January 1962, the band had succumbed to Epstein's charms and relentless pursuit of the band. Early auditions did not go down well, however, with the band's new manager lectured by the label Decca Records, "Guitar groups are on the way out, Mr. Epstein."

Sadly, when the band arrived back in Germany in April, Kirchherr, who met them at the airport distraught, delivered the news that Sutcliffe had died the day before of a brain hemorrhage.

Channeling their grief into their music, The Beatles were signed to EMI, under the Parlophone label. Epstein, who had continued to fail at landing the group a contract, did not sign The Beatles. It was Martin who secured the EMI deal. Martin had classical music training, an excellent ear as a producer, and coached The Beatles on their sound and songwriting. His close relationship and impact on the band's success would give him the kudos to be in contention for the title of 'Fifth Beatle' just as Epstein was.

Martin would later encourage orchestral contributions to The Beatles sounds and recordings, with Martin often playing piano, brass, and the organ. He also talked with McCartney about introducing a string quartet to the single Yesterday. He was a patient man when it came to the band's interest in drugs and pyschedelics, saying "Compared with Paul's songs, all of which seemed to keep in some sort of touch with reality, John's had a psychedelic, almost mystical quality ... John's imagery is one of the best things about his work – 'tangerine trees', 'marmalade skies', 'cellophane flowers'... I always saw him as an aural Salvador Dalí, rather than some drug-ridden record artist. On the other hand, I would be stupid to pretend that drugs didn't figure quite heavily in The Beatles' lives at that time ... they knew that I, in my schoolmasterly role, didn't approve ... Not only was I not into it myself, I couldn't see the need for it; and there's no doubt that, if I too had been on dope, Pepper would never have been the album it was. Perhaps it was the combination of dope and no dope that worked, who knows?"

Harrison later said of Martin's stabilizing and parental influence at the time: "I think we just grew through those years together, him as the straight man and us as the loonies; but he was always there for us to interpret our madness – we used to be slightly avant-garde on certain days of the week, and he would be there as the anchor person, to communicate that through the engineers and on to the tape."

Left to right: Stuart Sutcliffe, John Lennon, George Harrison - performing live onstage at the Top Ten Club

Drummer Ringo Starr performs onstage with Rory Storm & the Hurricanes at the Jive Hive

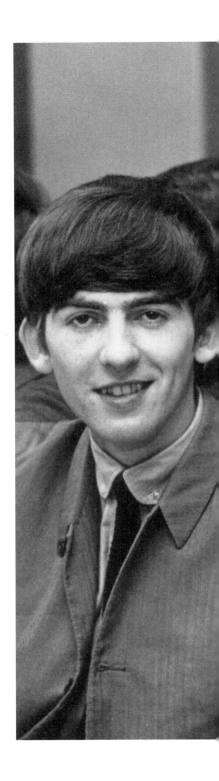

The first of many famous recordings at Abbey Road Studios in London, The Beatles set up under Martin's direction on June 6th, 1962.

Almost as soon as they were in session, Martin complained to Epstein of Best's standard of drumming. He suggested they use a session drummer in place of Best.

"It was a strictly professional decision. If he wasn't up to the mark...then there was no other choice."

– Paul McCartney on Pete Best's firing

In the middle of August, Ringo Starr left Rory Storm and the Hurricanes to join The Beatles as their drummer. Love Me Do was recorded in the studio in September with Starr on drums, which became the band's first single. Martin was still fussing over the drumming, though, and deviated with another drummer Andy White for the third session that followed. This third session produced Please Please Me and PS I Love You. Released in October, Love Me Do reached number 17 on the Record Retailer chart and their first television appearance, albeit on regional news, aired that same month.

A fourth studio session in November produced another recording of Please Please Me, with Martin declaring to the group "You've just made your first No.1." He was right.

"We always wanted every single record to have a different sound, we never wanted to get trapped in this THE Mersey beat."

– McCartney

The Fab Four in Sweden, 1963

The Beatles holding their silver LP and EP discs presented to them by EMI records in London to mark sales of records including the LP Please Please Me

Left to right; Ringo Starr on drums, George Harrison on guitar,
Paul McCartney on bass and vocals, and John Lennon on
acoustic guitars and vocals

By the end of 1962, The Beatles had finished their last residency in Hamburg. Lennon and McCartney had found a groove with their songwriting partnership and their popularity was rising.

In February 1963, the band recorded their first album, debuting with Please Please Me. The album was recorded in under 10 hours, with Lennon suffering the effects of a cold, which can be heard on close listening to the song Twist and Shout.

And while Epstein's attempt at signing the group was unsuccessful, he was successful in shaping the band's popularity and commercial appeal. He coached them on being more polished and professional, with Lennon remembering him advising, "'Look, if you really want to get in these bigger places, you're going to have to change – stop eating on stage, stop swearing, stop smoking.' We used to dress how we liked, on and off stage. He'd

tell us that jeans were not particularly smart and could we possibly manage to wear proper trousers, but he didn't want us suddenly looking square. He'd let us have our own sense of individuality."

Eventually, Lennon agreed saying, "I'll wear a bloody balloon if somebody's going to pay me."

Interestingly, around the same time the group had decided to bring a bit of uniformity to their live performances, presumably to get a more cohesive look and feel to their act. They agreed that they would each contribute to the vocals, including Starr who had reservations about his voice.

"They've got something! From Liverpool, I hear, of all places."

– quote from media at time of The Beatles' success, as featured in The Beatles Anthology

The Beatles jump for joy during a rehearsal for the Royal Command
Performance at the Prince of Wales Theatre

Following the group's departure from residency at the Cavern Club
in Liverpool and in Hamburg, their status in London was becoming
cult-like. By 1963, they were playing the Palladium, the Royal
Albert Hall, The Royal Variety Show.

For their Royal Variety Show performance, where of course
members of the British Royalty were present, Lennon teased the
audience, "For our next song, I'd like to ask for your help. For the
people in the cheaper seats, clap your hands ... and the rest of you,
if you'll just rattle your jewelry."

Of their hitting the big time, Lennon said, "We were just writing
songs ... pop songs with no more thought of them than that – to
create a sound. And the words were almost irrelevant."

Much later, in a 1987 interview, McCartney said the band all looked
up to Lennon, "He was like our own little Elvis ... We all looked up
to John. He was older and he was very much the leader; he was the
quickest wit and the smartest."

The Beatles looking sharp for the camera

The Beatles in Liverpool, 1962

Beatlemania

" I have never seen anything like it. Nor heard any noise to approximate the ceaseless, frantic, hysterical scream which met The Beatles when they took the stage after what seemed a hundred years of earlier acts. All very good, all marking time, because no one had come for anything other than The Beatles...

"Then the theatre went wild. First aid men and police – men in the stalls, women mainly in the balcony – taut and anxious, patrolled the aisles, one to every three rows.

"Many girls fainted. Thirty were gently carried out, protesting in their hysteria, forlorn and wretched in an unrequited love for four lads who might have lived next door.

"The stalls were like a nightmare March Fair. No one could remain seated. Clutching each other, hurling jelly babies at the stage, beating their brows, the youth of Britain's second city surrendered themselves totally."

– *Derek Taylor, Fifty Years Adrift*

During that same recording of their debut album Please Please Me The Beatles laid down ten songs in just one session. The title track was issued two months ahead of the album, and just as Martin predicted, came in at Number One.

Lennon said that he and McCartney were "just writing songs à la Everly Brothers, à la Buddy Holly, pop songs with no more thought of them than that – to create a sound. And the words were almost irrelevant."

After the album was released in March, the group's third single From Me to You followed in April, another chart topper that kicked off what would be a string of Number One Singles in the UK. 16 Number Ones would be released over the next six years, beginning what would be termed Beatlemania.

Police link arms to control the frenzied queue for Beatles tickets in Lewisham, south London

The Beatles climb on to a bus at London Airport, George Harrison capturing the moment on film with a cine-camera

Paul McCartney waves from a taxi on the Champs Elysees, Paris, France

According to reports, it was Canadian reporter Sandy Gardiner who dubbed the phenomenon 'Beatlemania' using the term in the Ottawa Journal, November 1963.

The band's fourth single She Loves You set the record for the fastest sales of any record in the UK, with 750,000 sold in just under a four-week period. It went on to become their first single to sell a million copies.

"John and I wrote it together. We were in a van up in Newcastle somewhere and we'd just gone over to our hotel. I originally got an idea of doing one of those answering songs, where a couple of us sing about 'she loves you' ...and the other one sort of says the 'yes, yes' bit. You know, 'yeah yeah' answering whoever is saying it. But we decided that was a crummy idea anyway. But we had the idea to write a song called 'She Loves You' then. And we just sat up in the hotel bedroom for a few hours and wrote it, you know."
– Paul McCartney, 1963

"We rehearsed the end bit of 'She Loves You' and took it to George. And he just laughed and said, 'Well, you can't do the end of course... that sixth... it's too like the Andrew Sisters.' We just said, 'Alright, we'll try it without,' and we tried it and it wasn't as good. Then he conceded, 'You're right, I guess.' But we were both very flexible. We would listen to George's ideas too, because he was a producer and a musician, and he obviously knew what he was talking about. There was good to-and-fro. We loved that bit, and we rehearsed it a lot. John and I wrote that in a hotel room, on twin beds during an afternoon off – I mean, God bless their little cotton socks, those boys WORKED! Here I am talking about an afternoon off, and we're sitting there writing! We just loved it so much. It wasn't work."
– Paul McCartney, 1988

As to be expected, with such commercial success came a lot of media attention. Their nonchalant, slightly uninterested response to the media, along with their Liverpudlian sense of humor only served to pique media interest.

At the same time, the public's interest in the group started to gain momentum and in the same way their idol Elvis Presley was greeted with screaming, fainting, hysterical fans, now the Fab Four faced Beatlemania everywhere they went.

A screaming American music fan is gripped by Beatlemania as the band perform onstage at Carnegie Hall, New York

Screaming Beatles fans holding banners and waving at band

Six months after they first topped the charts, The Beatles commenced a short tour of Sweden, which was their first overseas engagement since their Hamburg residency. By December, on their return, they landed at Heathrow airport to torrential rain and a heavy reception from hundreds of screaming fans. More Beatlemania followed.

According to reports, more than a hundred incidences like this were to follow, with hoards of screaming fans accompanied by journalists and photographers, descending on The Beatles at every point.

An intense nine-month tour of Britain heightened The Beatles' fan worship and hysteria. In November, police used high-pressured water hoses to control the crowds at a concert in Plymouth.

Unbelievably, the single that launched their success, Please Please Me stayed at Number One for 30 weeks.

Demonstrating they were now officially and firmly the rock gods of the UK, their own single With The Beatles bumped it off the spot. Supported by slicker studio production, With The Beatles held the top spot for 21 weeks, and stayed in the charts for 40 weeks. With critics describing this as much better than the original, the album secured Lennon and McCartney acclaim.

Critic William Mann of The Times, described the duo as "the outstanding English composers of 1963." The broadsheet then published a series of articles reviewing in detail their music, which brought credibility to the group's music. Now the second album in UK chart history to sell a million copies, the band's press officer, Tony Barrow, coined the term 'fabulous foursome', which the media widely adopted as the 'Fab Four.'

*Left to right; Paul McCartney & John Lennon
rehearsing onstage during American tour*

As EMI's American arm, Capitol Records initially declined to use The Beatles and to release their music in the States. They did not issue the first three singles, and while negotiations were being made with two other independent US labels, issues with the royalties and rights under EMI/Capitol meant discussions ground to a halt. This was not before the singles were released in the States in 1963; however, the lack of marketing potential meant the singles did not receive much in the way of attention.

Then, Esptein stepped up his game and proved his genius as manager and secured a £27,600 ($40,000) marketing campaign and the backing of DJ Carrol James, who became the first to play The Beatles in December in 1963. What followed was a surge in demand for the group on other radio networks, and so Capitol were proved wrong and rushed out the release of I Want to Hold Your Hand that same month. It sold a million copies and hit Number One in the US by mid-January of 1964.

A week before Valentine's Day, The Beatles landed in the US to romance fans. With an estimated 4,000 fans sending them off at Heathrow airport, The Beatles landed to be greeted by another 3,000 fans in New York's John F. Kennedy International Airport. Just two days later, the band met another 73 million viewers via the television show that helped launch Elvis Presley's career, The Ed Sullivan Show. Although the US critics deflated the reception somewhat with negative reviews, the band still went to Washington for their first US concert and witnessed more Beatlemania. In New York the next day, they received more positive reception from fans at the two shows they played. The Beatles were not a flash in the pan. And another 70 million viewers who tuned in to watch The Beatles' second appearance on The Ed Sullivan Show defied the critics.

Capitol Records must have been regretting their earlier dismissal of the group. Especially when United Artists Records circled the group offering them a movie deal with soundtrack options for a series of three films. After the mock-documentary A Hard Day's Night was released, they welcomed international commercial success and critical acclaim. The soundtrack was seen as evidence the group's sound had matured.

The Beatles pose in the sea at Miami Beach during the band's tour of America

The Beatles, performing on The Ed Sullivan Show February 9, 1964

The title track was so different to what had been heard before, that debate over the opening chord played by Harrison (on his 12-string Rickenbacker guitar) was never agreed on, until a mathematician claimed a solution in 2008.

Many musicians and scholars had claimed theories on what chord was played and why it was difficult to ascertain. Jason Brown, of the University of Dalhousie's Department of Mathematics (also a guitar and music fan) decided to solve it mathematically. Applying a calculation called the Fourier Transform, Brown deconstructed the frequencies using computer software, parsing out the notes. The frequencies did not match the instruments.

"George played a 12-string Rickenbacker, Lennon had his six string, Paul had his bass…none of them quite fit what I found," he explains. "Then the solution hit me: it wasn't just those instruments. There was a piano in there as well, and that accounted for the problematic frequencies."

Dr. Brown said Martin must have also played, adding another piano chord impossible to play in the guitar. The chord that resulted was so different to anything heard before; the mathematician received international attention and proved once again the uniqueness of The Beatles and their experimental approach to music.

At this point, The Beatles held 12 spots on the Hot 100 singles chart, and they successfully paved the way for British acts to follow to the States, termed 'The British Invasion.'

Top: Paul McCartney performing with The Beatles during their US tour, August 1965

Above: The Beatles backstage at Fairfield Halls, Croydon, April 25th, 1963

After completing their tour of 23 American cities with hectic success, The Beatles flew from John F. Kennedy International Airport for England

Left to right; Paul McCartney, George Harrison, John Lennon, and Ringo Starr of The Beatles show off their MBE Awards after the presentation at Buckingham Palace, 1965

*Beatles fans try to break through a police line at Buckingham
Palace in London where the group were due to receive MBEs*

With a grueling international tour that followed, The
Beatles survived thirty-seven shows over twenty-
seven days in Denmark, the Netherlands, Hong
Kong, Australia, and New Zealand. The next month,
they conducted a thirty-concert tour of twenty-
three cities in the US. At each point, Beatlemania
was present, with between 10,000 and 20,000 fans
appearing at each thirty-minute performance.

Martin would not have been best pleased at The
Beatles' further experimentation with recreational
drugs during this time. It was apparently while
they were in New York that the group met Bob
Dylan, who introduced them to cannabis, or 'dope'.
Interestingly, though, it appeared it was not just
Dylan's drug choice that influenced them, for
Lennon would later be adopting vocal tones and
impressions of Dylan in recording sessions.

In addition to the introduction of cannabis by Dylan,
The Beatles were also inadvertently introduced to
LSD while at a dinner. In what would be considered

an outrageous move by today's standards, Lennon
and Harrison's dentist had spiked their coffees.

In the middle of Beatlemania, commercial success,
and drug experimentation, for many it came as a
bit of a shock when Queen Elizabeth II appointed
all four Beatles Members of the Order of the
British Empire (MBE) after Prime Minister Harold
Wilson nominated them for the award. Several
Conservatives who had received the same Order
returned theirs in protest. It was the middle of 1965.

The soundtrack to the group's second film, Help!
was mostly written and sung by Lennon, including
the much-loved title song Ticket to Ride.

The group then embarked on a third tour of the US with an opening performance in August to a world-record breaking audience of 55,600 people at Shea Stadium in New York. Considered by some the group's most well known concerts, The Beatles went on to deliver another nine packed out shows. Following this, the band was invited to meet their musical hero Elvis, at his home in his Beverly Hills mansion. Tony Barrow, the group's publicist recalled the following story to BBC News Entertainment reporter Ian Youngs:

"When I put the idea of meeting Elvis to John, Paul, George, and Ringo, they were initially put off by the fact that the press might be involved. I remember George saying, 'If this is going to be another dirty big publicity circus, let's forget it.' They did want to meet their rock 'n' roll idol, but not with a gang of reporters and photographers around to hassle them. The first fundamental ground rules to be set were: no press to be invited, no pictures to be taken, no recordings to be made, and no leaking of our plans in advance.

'It was shortly before 10pm when we drove over. We were in a convoy of three big black limousines, led by [Elvis' manager] Colonel Parker and his people. The property consisted of two storeys nestled into a hillside. It was a vast, round building with a lot of windows and a spacious front garden. There was a Rolls Royce and a couple of Cadillacs lining the drive.

'Members of the famous 'Memphis Mafia' guarded the tall gates but they waved our line of limousines straight through. Once inside the front door, our feet seemed to sink inches into deep white shag pile carpeting. We arrived in the center of the building, into this massive circular room bathed in red and blue light, and this was where the King entertained.

The Beatles discuss their upcoming Shea Stadium concert at a press conference

The Beatles perform at Shea Stadium, New York on August 15th, 1965

The Fab Four in Sweden, 1963

"This was Elvis Presley's giant playpen, complete with a color television, a jukebox, a deep crescent-shaped couch, a couple of pool and games tables, and a well-stocked bar. I would say, at a guess, that Presley's army of henchmen and their womenfolk must have totaled about 20 people, well outnumbering our little group.

"As the two teams faced one another, there was a weird silence and it was John who spoke first, rather awkwardly blurting out a stream of questions at Elvis, saying: 'Why do you do all these soft-centered ballads for the cinema these days? What happened to good old rock 'n' roll?'

"Elvis was fairly quiet – that was my first reaction. He smiled a lot and shook hands with everybody. The ice didn't really break in the early stages at all. The boys and Elvis swapped tour stories, but it hadn't got going. Music was their natural meeting point, their most intelligent means of communication.

"They quickly exhausted their initial bout of small talk and there was this embarrassing silence between the mega-famous five, stood there facing each other, with very little of import being said.

"Apart from anything else, I think it was just that each was in awe of the other. Elvis didn't have that much confidence, as far as I could see. He was a fairly easily embarrassed person by the look of him.

Elvis invited The Beatles to jam with him at Graceland

*Elvis Presley strolls the grounds
of his Graceland estate*

"But Elvis suddenly plugged the gap by calling for some guitars to be handed out to John, Paul, and George, and a piano was hauled into view. Up to that point, the party really had been a bit lifeless and unexciting. But as soon as Presley and The Beatles began to play together, the atmosphere livened up.

"The boys found that they could make much better conversation with their guitars than they could with their spoken word. Music was their natural meeting point, their most intelligent means of communication.

"I can't remember all the things that they played but I do remember one of the songs was I Feel Fine. And I remember Ringo, who of course didn't have an instrument, tapping out the backbeat with his fingers on the nearest bits of wooden furniture.

"Everybody was singing. Elvis strummed a few bass guitar chords for Paul and said: 'See, I'm practicing.' And Paul came back with some quip about: 'Don't worry, between us, me and Brian Epstein will make a star of you soon.'

"It would be wonderful to have either photographs or recordings. That recording would be invaluable, surely. It would be a multi-million dollar piece of tape. But it wasn't to be. It was an amazing session to listen to.

*The Beatles holding the Union Jack on the steps
going up to an airplane at London Airport, 1964*

"Parker and Epstein lost interest - they were leaving the children to play. Parker put his plump arm around Brian Epstein's shoulder and led him away to a quiet corner of this playroom. Epstein at this point grabbed his chance to bring up the subject he'd been waiting to raise, which was his secret agenda. He hoped to persuade Parker to let him present Elvis in a series of UK concerts.

"It was a hopeless project from the outset, although at the time, Parker pretended to leave the door open by saying he'd think about it. The party ended when Colonel Parker decided that it was time for it to end. He started dishing out presents, which mostly consisted of piles of Elvis Presley albums.

"I remember, as we went out to our limousines, John put on his Adolf Hitler accent and shouted: 'Long live ze king.' Also, John said, as we got into our limousines: 'Elvis was stoned.' George Harrison responded very quietly: 'Aren't we all?'

"They tried to make light of it and not show too much adoration for their idol, but Elvis Presley was their idol and one of the prime influences of The Beatles' music."

By October 1965, in the middle of Beatlemania, the group was back in the recording studio.

For the first time in more than a year, The Beatles had a block of time without live shows or commitments to appearances. Critically acclaimed Rubber Soul was the product of a couple of months in session, demonstrating the band's maturity again with a deeper, more soulful and romantic musical direction. Some reviewers and writers have credited this to their now regular use of cannabis, which seemed to be supported by the band's commentary, with Lennon labeling it "the pot album." Starr said, "Grass was really influential in a lot of our changes, especially with the writers. And because they were writing different material, we were playing differently."

Beatles Rubber Soul album cover

Paul McCartney (left) and John Lennon perform on stage at the Washington Coliseum, Washington DC, February 11th, 1964

This more artful, romantic approach was described by Lennon when he talked of the song Norwegian Wood, "I was trying to be sophisticated in writing about an affair ... but in such a smokescreen way that you couldn't tell."

Again, the combination of Lennon-McCartney's songwriting on this album meant two things – musical brilliance and commercial success. Unfortunately, however, it also signaled the point at which the pair's competitiveness began to create brotherly friction. Where the duo shared credit for the incredible songwriting on the album and the hit song In My Life, each later claimed to be the main writer of the song. Sadly, the relationship between the two was beginning to sour, with recording engineer Norman Smith noticing, "the clash between John and Paul was becoming obvious… and as far as Paul was concerned, George could do no right."

Despite the relationship tension within the band, their image and success was at its peak. They were, however, embarking on new, more adventurous imagery and sounds on their albums. The squeaky clean, suited and booted Beatles launched in the early sixties, with a conventional looking logo (which was designed by Ivor Arbiter, a designer and instrument retailer), was about to undergo a metamorphosis.

In June of 1966, the album Yesterday and Today displayed a controversial image on its cover. A compilation album for the US by Capitol Records, it showed The Beatles smiling, dressed in butcher's overalls, surrounded by red, raw meat and toy baby dolls with limbs mutilated.

Because of the fuss, thousands of copies had a new cover stuck over the top of the controversial original image. Some critics and analysts suggest the imagery symbolized Capitol's "butchering" of their US releases. In 2005, a 'first-edition' unpeeled copy of this album was auctioned for $10,500 (£7,250.00).

'The Butcher' version of
the album cover

McCartney (left) and Lennon during
their American tour, August 1965

More controversy followed. In the Philippines, while on tour, Imelda Marcos, the then-First Lady, invited the band to a breakfast reception at the Presidential Palace. Epstein, in accordance with their usual policy of declining official invitations, politely said the group was unable to attend. Considered an insult, with Marcos unaccustomed to being declined, the group had offended the nation and riots broke out. They eventually managed to leave the Philippines, but not before being scared by the chaos that resulted from their innocent actions. It was not an easy departure from the country.

On returning home, the group were exposed to yet more controversy.

American religious and conservative groups were furious over comments Lennon had made to a British reporter, Maureen Cleave, in an interview in March of '66, "Christianity will go," Lennon said. "It will vanish and shrink. I needn't argue about that; I'm right and I will be proved right. We're more popular than Jesus now; I don't know which will go first, rock 'n' roll or Christianity. Jesus was alright but his disciples were thick and ordinary. It's them twisting it that ruins it for me."

Going largely undetected in the UK, his comments had resurfaced in a US teenage fan magazine Datebook, which had re-printed his comments some five months later. Ironically, this was on the eve of the August US tour.

The media storm went global, and Spanish and Dutch stations banned their music, along with the South African broadcasting service. The Vatican issued a protest. In response, Epstein declared Lennon's words were taken out of context.

Lennon said, "If I'd said television was more popular than Jesus, I might have got away with it," and claimed he had meant the comment in relation to how people perceived their success. At that same press conference, when pressured by reporters, he said, "If you want me to apologize, if that will make you happy, then okay, I'm sorry."

Lennon after making a formal apology for his controversial statement that the group were 'more popular than Jesus'

Photo of The Beatles and Brian Epstein arriving back at Heathrow from their Far East Tour ending in Manila.

The August US tour would become their last. Having had enough of trying to overcome the volume of the screams from audiences, The Beatles were tired of performing live, only to have their music drowned out.

A week before their final tour, The Beatles released Revolver, to more critical acclaim. Just one of many music reviewers rating it as a brilliant album, Pitchfork Media's writer Scott Plagenhoef described it, "the sound of a band growing into supreme confidence" and "redefining what was expected from popular music."

Another step forward in experimental music making, the album showcased sophisticated songwriting and a new range of styles, including classical string arrangements and psychedelic rock. However, to the band, the difference was not so apparent.

"I don't see too much difference myself in Rubber Soul and Revolver. To me they could both be like volume one and volume two. They both were very pleasant and enjoyable records for me."
– *George Harrison*

Taking leave from its typical group image of the band on the front cover, it featured one designed by a friend of the band, Klaus Voorman. Its arty cover matched the new direction the band was taking musically.

The single pre-released before the album was Paperback Writer. Short films were released for the single, along with Rain, and after airing on television shows such as Top Of The Pops, were considered the first of what would become standard in the music industry – the music video.

The album cover for Revolver designed by artist Klaus Voorman, which was released on August 6th, 1966

The Beatles on Top of the Pops, 1966

Paul McCartney, Ringo Starr, John Lennon,
and George Harrison at Top Of The Pops

Further avant-garde songs included Tomorrow Never Knows, which was said to have been inspired by Lennon's reading of Timothy Leary's The Psychedelic Experience: A Manual Based on the Tibetan Book of the Dead.

"[Timothy] Leary was the one who was going round saying, 'Take it, take it, take it,' and we followed his instructions in The Book of the Dead, his how-to-take-a-trip book. I did it just like he said in the book, and then I wrote 'Tomorrow Never Knows,' which is almost the first acid song, 'Lay down all thought, surrender to the void.' I took one of Ringo's malapropisms as the title.

'Tomorrow Never Knows' ... I didn't know what I was saying and you just find out later. I know that when there are some lyrics I dig, I know that somewhere people will be looking at them."

– John Lennon, 1968

Using experimental techniques, it was created by distributing eight tape decks around the EMI building, where an engineer would randomly vary the movement of the tape loop. Martin then created a recording of the samples in a composite.

*John Lennon (on tambourine) with
record producer George Martin*

The Beatles; 1960s

*The Beatles disembark from an airplane at London Airport
in the early morning, on return from their American tour*

Another completely unique recording was discovered in Eleanor Rigby, the track that featured a string octet. And Harrison also had a chance to display his considerable talents on this album. Three of his singles appeared on the record and later declared it his favourite album.

Others agreed. Rolling Stone magazine voted it the third greatest album of all time in 2003.

Writer Chris Ingham said the tracks were "studio creations ... and there was no way a four-piece rock 'n' roll group could do them justice, particularly through the desensitizing wall of the fans' screams. 'Live Beatles' and 'Studio Beatles' had become entirely different beasts."

The decision to end live shows was arguably good for the group. Incredibly, they had performed more than 1,400 concert shows across the globe in a small four-year window. It must have been exhausting.

On the last show, in San Francisco on August 29th, 1966, the band left the Beatlemania period behind. They were now free to venture into more experimental musical directions.

Sgt. Pepper's Lonely Hearts Club Band, vinyl LP record,1967

The Beatles celebrate the completion of their new album, Sgt. Pepper's Lonely Hearts Club Band

After a few months' rest, the group went back to the studio in November to record Sgt. Pepper's Lonely Hearts Club Band.

Engineer Geoff Emerick claimed the recording took over 700 hours, a far cry from their early days of ten-hour recordings. At this point, the group was determined to be different. Emerick said the band insisted, "that everything on Sgt. Pepper had to be different. We had microphones right down in the bells of brass instruments and headphones turned into microphones attached to violins. We used giant primitive oscillators to vary the speed of instruments and vocals and we had tapes chopped to pieces and stuck together upside down and the wrong way around."

"It was an idea I had, I think, when I was flying from LA to somewhere. I thought it would be nice to lose our identities, to submerge ourselves in the persona of a fake group. We would make up all the culture around it and collect all our heroes in one place. So I thought, a typical stupid-sounding name for a Dr. Hook's Medicine Show and Traveling Circus kind of thing would be 'Sgt. Pepper's Lonely Hearts Club Band.' Just a word game, really."

– *Paul McCartney, 1984*

"Paul wrote it after a trip to America. The whole west coast long named group thing was coming in, you know, when people were no longer called The Beatles or the Crickets, they were suddenly Fred and His Incredible Shrinking Grateful Airplanes. He got influenced by that and came up with this idea of doing us as somebody else. He was trying to put something between The Beatles and the public. It took the 'I' out of it some. Like the early days, saying 'She loves you' instead of 'I love you.' So that's the song."

– *John Lennon, 1980*

The inside of the vinyl cover for the album
Sgt. Pepper's Lonely Hearts Club Band

*The Beatles at the press launch for their new
album Sgt. Pepper's Lonely Hearts Club Band*

A street sign for Penny Lane, Liverpool – the inspiration for the Beatles' famous song

What followed was a complex couple of releases. Featuring a 40-piece orchestra, Strawberry Fields Forever/Penny Lane was a double single release in February. The LP followed this, somewhat slowly, in June. Considering they were recorded on old school four-tracks, the musical acclaim for the releases was astonishing and globally agreed. This critical acclaim was matched by the opinions of their contemporaries and future musicians. It inspired generations of formatted and manipulated sounds in rock and pop.

It was declared a masterpiece. It had surpassed the Elvis revolution by creating a new sound and, technically, a new genre or sub-genre within rock.

In Strawberry Fields, Lennon revisited his youth, and drew on his memories of his playing in the garden of a Salvation Army children's home. One of the most famous images of music albums, the imagery on the album was also symbolic of the change The Beatles would put the music industry through and, themselves. Designed by pop artists Peter Blake and Jann Haworth, the cover image showed the band members as the fictional group in the title track. Cultural historian Jonathan Harris described their costumes as "brightly colored parodies of military uniforms" as a knowingly "anti-authoritarian and anti-establishment" display.

Among those featured on the cover of Sgt. Pepper's Lonely Hearts Club Band are Stuart Sutcliffe, Laurel and Hardy, Marilyn Monroe, Karl Marx, boxer Sonny Liston, Bob Dylan, Lenny Bruce, and Shirley Temple. According to reports, Mae West did not originally grant permission to the band for use of her image on the album, although she later changed her mind when they each wrote her a note explaining how much it would mean to them. Shirley Temple was the only personality who asked to listen to the album before agreeing to their use of her image.

It was also the first major rock album to put its lyrics on the back cover, which meant fans could pour over them and learn them by heart. It also meant they were analyzed over and over by critics, scholars, and fans. McCartney said, "We write songs. We know what we mean by them. But in a week someone else says something about it and you can't deny it. ... You put your own meaning at your own level to our songs."

Paul McCartney conducts a 41-piece orchestra during recording sessions for Sgt. Pepper's Lonely Hearts Club Band

The Beatles hold the sleeve of their new LP,
Sgt. Pepper's Lonely Hearts Club Band

The Beatles perform their song 'All You Need Is Love' the first live satellite uplink performance broadcast to the world on June 25, 1967

The Beatles sporting multi-lingual Love Is All You Need sandwich boards

Despite the group not taking the album to concert performances, they followed Elvis' direction with live global televised performances, taking their single All you Need is Love to 350 million viewers around the world.

"I think if you get down to basics, whatever the problem is, it's usually to do with love. So I think 'All You Need is Love' is a true statement. I'm not saying, 'All you have to do is...' because 'All You Need' came out in the Flower Power Generation time. It doesn't mean that all you have to do is put on a phoney smile or wear a flower dress and it's gonna be alright. Love is not just something that you stick on posters or stick on the back of your car, or on the back of your jacket or on a badge. I'm talking about real love, so I still believe that. Love is appreciation of other people and allowing them to be. Love is allowing somebody to be themselves and that's what we do need."

– John Lennon, 1971

It became the anthem to the Summer of Love.

The iconic Abbey Road album cover

John Lennon

John Lennon at home in Liverpool during his schooldays, circa 1950

K nown worldwide as one half of the most celebrated songwriting partnership ever and a spokesman for world peace, John Lennon came from modest beginnings.

Born October 9th, 1940 in Liverpool, John Winston Lennon's mother was Julia and father Alfred, a seaman who was away when his son was born. John's first name came from his paternal grandfather and his middle name from the then-Prime Minister of Britain, Winston Churchill. His father sent checks to support his son's upbringing, to his wife at 9 Newcastle Road, Liverpool. When Lennon was four years old, his father went absent without leave and the checks stopped arriving. It was reported that his father came back after six months and offered to support the family, but his mother was by now pregnant with another man's child.

Lennon's aunt, Mimi Smith, his mother's sister, had reported them to Social Services twice, and at one point Lennon was given to Smith to raise him. His troubled family continued, when his father came to visit Smith over a year later. At just five years of age, Lennon was forced to choose between his parents following a heated argument. His father had taken Lennon to Blackpool, and his mother followed them after she'd discovered his father had intended to emigrate to New Zealand. She asked his son to choose between them. He apparently chose his father, saying it out loud two times, but as his mother walked away he cried and followed her.

Lennon would be 25 years old before he would next see his father.

John Lennon with his mother, Julia,
at Ardmore, Rockferry, Cheshire

John Lennon at his home sitting on a wall

Lennon lived and was raised at 251 Menlove Avenue in Woolton, Liverpool, his aunt Mimi and Uncle George's home. The Smiths had no children of their own and they would treat him as their own. His aunt bought him volumes of short stories and taught him crossword puzzles as part of his leisure time. Lennon's mother would visit regularly and when he turned 11, he would also visit her at her home at 1 Blomfield Road. His mother taught him the banjo and played him Elvis Presley records. From his mother, he learned to play Fats Domino's Ain't That a Shame.

"Part of me would like to be accepted by all facets of society and not be this loudmouthed lunatic poet/musician. But I cannot be what I am not ... I was the one who all the other boys' parents – including Paul's father – would say, 'Keep away from him'... The parents instinctively recognized I was a troublemaker, meaning I did not conform and I would influence their children, which I did. I did my best to disrupt every friend's home ... Partly out of envy that I didn't have this so-called home ... but I did... There were five women that were my family. Five strong, intelligent, beautiful women, five sisters. One happened to be my mother. [She] just couldn't deal with life. She was the youngest and she had a husband who ran away to sea and the war was on and she couldn't cope with me, and I ended up living with her elder sister. Now those women were fantastic ... And that was my first feminist education ... I would infiltrate the other boys minds. I could say, 'Parents are not gods because I don't live with mine and, therefore, I know.'"

– Lennon on his family life, 1980

Fats Domino, a major influence on a young John Lennon

Lennon was 14 when his uncle died of a liver hemorrhage in the summer of 1955. It was the first of more family tragedy to come. Raised an Anglican, young Lennon went to Dovedale Primary School and from 1952 for the following five years, he attended Quarry Bank High School in Liverpool.

He was described a good-natured boy, who had a sense of humor and artistic talent. He created a school magazine called The Daily Howl, for which he drew cartoons. However, his school reports were less complimentary, "Certainly on the road to failure... hopeless... rather a clown in class... wasting other pupils' time."

In 1956, his mother gave Lennon his first guitar, although the gift had conditions. She would 'lend' him five pounds and ten shillings to return the guitar to her house, as she was aware Lennon's aunt would not approve. Indeed, his aunt told him, 'The guitar's all very well, John, but you'll never make a living out of it.'

In 1958, when Lennon was 17, his mother was killed. She was walking home from visiting the Smith's house and was hit by a car. It is no surprise that this would have a big impact on the young musician. Indeed, Lennon continued with his poor behavior, especially around authority, where he displayed a rebellious streak.

Lennon failed his O-level exams in high school. He was accepted in the Liverpool College of Art after his aunt and headmaster made a case for him and his circumstances.

Top; John Lennon portrait, 1960

Above; Lennon riding a bicycle during the 1960s

Lennon makes his performing debut in 1960

Lennon's behavior did not improve. His rejection of authority extended to Art College. In fact, he was so disruptive to the classes that he was excluded from a painting class and a graphic arts course. He was also threatened with expulsion after he sat on a life class nude model while the students attempted to complete their life drawings.

In his final year, he was thrown out of college after failing the final exam.

It was at the Liverpool College of Art that Lennon met his first wife Cynthia Powell. Powell was attracted to Lennon, even though she was engaged to another man and was reportedly slightly frightened of him. She'd heard that he was fond of Brigitte Bardot, the sultry French actress, so she dyed her hair blonde. She described being

scared of his attitude, and recalls when Lennon eventually asked her out and she told him she was engaged, he screamed out, "I didn't ask you to f*****' marry me, did I?"

As Lennon had by now established the Quarrymen, and Powell often joined him at the gigs and when the band established themselves as The Beatles, she traveled with McCartney's then girlfriend to Hamburg to visit. Powell remembers him as aggressive, angry, and jealous. Lennon himself later said he wrote Getting Better about his realization of his abusive behavior towards women, "I used to be cruel to my woman, and physically – any woman. I was a hitter. I couldn't express myself and I hit. I fought men and I hit women. That is why I am always on about peace."

The Quarrymen perform onstage at their first concert at the Casbah Coffee House

John with his first wife Cynthia, at London Airport

Cynthia Lennon outside the Royal Courts of Justice in London, where she started divorce proceedings in 1968

In July of 1962, Powell told Lennon she was pregnant, to which he replied, "There's only one thing for it Cyn. We'll have to get married." Married at the register office in Liverpool, by this point Beatlemania was beginning to really take shape. Epstein told the couple to keep it secret; he was concerned the fans would not like a married band member. Julian Lennon was born April 8th, 1963 when his father was on tour. He first saw his son at three days old.

Powell famously discovered Lennon in bed with Yoko Ono, the Japanese conceptual artist he would later marry. Although there are differing accounts of how Lennon and Ono met, the most popular story was that they met at an art gallery in London where Ono was showing her conceptual art. After Ono started calling Lennon's home, Powell asked him why she kept phoning – he explained to his wife that Ono was only after money for her art.

In May 1968, while Powell was on vacation, Lennon invited Ono to visit. They reportedly spent the night recording the Two Virgins album, staying up all-night and then "made love at dawn." It was said that when his wife returned home, she found Ono wearing her bathrobe and drinking tea with Lennon who simply said, "Oh, hi."

Shortly after, Powell and Lennon settled their divorce out of court, with Powell granted custody of Julian and £100,000 settlement.

Yoko Ono, working as an artist in London in 1964

John Lennon and his wife Yoko Ono
with Yoko's daughter Kyoko in 1969

Following his divorce from Cynthia in 1968 John Lennon married the Japanese avant-garde artist Yoko Ono in March 1969

After Lennon married Ono in 1969, he changed his name to John Ono Lennon and had a son with Ono, Sean. Lennon issued a series of lithographs titled Bag One, which showcased revealing shots of the couple from their honeymoon. Eight out of 14 of the images were determined to be indecent and confiscated.

Lennon disbanded the band that same year, but agreed not to share it with the media until the contract was renegotiated. However, McCartney announced his own departure on releasing his debut solo album in April 1970. Lennon reportedly said, "Jesus Christ! He gets all the credit for it!"

He later said, "I started the band. I disbanded it. It's as simple as that." In interviews, he described his annoyance with McCartney at using the break up to advance his own solo record sales and he also described what he considered to be the hostility of band members towards Ono.

Following the band's break up, Lennon led a successful solo career, with critically acclaimed albums John Lennon/Plastic Ono Band and Imagine, which captured the hearts of music fans through singles Give Peace a Chance and Imagine. After a period of quiet from the music industry, much later, in 1980, Lennon resurfaced in the music world with Ono, recording the album Double Fantasy.

Lennon and Ono became famous for their 'Bed-in for Peace' activism and actively protested against the Vietnam War. Lennon had also returned his MBE to the Queen in protest at Britain's involvement in the Nigerian Civil War.

"John's in love with Yoko and he's no longer in love with the other three of us."

– Paul McCartney to the Evening Standard, April 1970

Following the band's break up, Lennon and Ono lived together in London and New York. Because of the drug charges against Lennon, he was concerned about deportation from America. It was reported that the pressures of that and Ono's separation from her daughter (from a previous marriage) meant the couple separated in 1973. The couple reconciled in 1975 and that same year, Ono gave birth to Sean.

Lennon's solo album sales were huge. It was recorded in 2012 that in the US alone, he sold more than 14 million units. He was responsible for 25 number one songs on the Hot 100 and was posthumously inducted into the Songwriters Hall of Fame in 1987 and into the Rock and Roll Hall of Fame in 1994.

Top; John Lennon poses for a photo with his wife Yoko Ono and son Sean Lennon in 1977 in New York City

John Lennon and Yoko Ono pose on the steps of the Apple building in London, holding one of the posters that they distributed to the world's major cities

The couple were staging a 'bed-in for peace' and stayed in bed for seven days "as a protest against war and violence in the world"

*John and Yoko at a
rally in Hyde Park,
London, 1975*

Paul McCartney

Along with Lennon, McCartney was famed for his songwriting talents and as part of the duo, had, and continues to have, a global fan base. Born on June 18th, 1942 James Paul McCartney to Mary and James, he also had a modest upbringing. Like Lennon, McCartney's father was absent from his birth due to his role as a volunteer firefighter in World War II. With one younger brother, Michael, and both parents earning an income, he had a more stable and comfortable early childhood than his songwriting partner.

Attending school from 1947 at Stockton Wood Road, he was later transferred to Joseph William Junior School due to overcrowding at Stockton. In 1953, McCartney passed his exams (along with only three other students, out of the 90 children sitting them). He was granted a place at the Liverpool Institute, which was how he met George Harrison. Harrison and McCartney got the bus together to the Institute and they quickly formed a friendship. McCartney said: "I tended to talk down to him, because he was a year younger."

With his father away at war, McCartney's mother was the breadwinner, working as a midwife, which secured them a home at 20 Forthlin Road in Allerton, where he grew up. McCartney recalled his mother having to ride her bicycle to patients, on one occasion she left "about three in the morning [the] streets ... thick with snow."

Paul McCartney with his brother in 1948

In a strange twist of fate, McCartney had lost his mother at a young age, just as Lennon did. His mother died when he was just 14. Suffering an embolism, a fatal blood clot, McCartney was then raised by his father in his teenage years.

As a bandleader for Jim Mac's Jazz Band in the 1920s, his father was an accomplished trumpet player and pianist. He encouraged both of his sons musically, and gave his eldest a trumpet for his 14th birthday. After falling in love with rock and roll, he traded it for an acoustic guitar worth £15 at the time. Discovering he found it difficult to play right handed, McCartney was inspired by Slim Whitman's left handed playing and reversed the strings. McCartney wrote his first song playing that guitar (I Lost My Little Girl) and another on the piano, which would late be developed into When I'm Sixty Four.

Just a year later, McCartney met Lennon and his band The Quarrymen. Having found some confidence singing and performing at a Butlin's Holiday Camp talent competition, where he sang Long Tall Sally, McCartney impressed Lennon. He was heavily influenced by rhythm and blues, with Little Richard his hero.

"If I couldn't have any other instrument, I would have to have an acoustic guitar."
– McCartney, Guitar Player, July 1990

A pre-Beatle Paul McCartney at home in Liverpool, 1956

1960 Gibson Les Paul Standard left-handed model guitar owned by Paul McCartney

The council house in Liverpool which was home to Sir Paul McCartney's family

Paul McCartney and his dog, Martha, 1960

In addition to Little Richard, McCartney shared musical taste with Lennon and was a fan of Elvis Presley, Buddy Holly, Carl Perkins, and Chuck Berry. He said of the bass line in I Saw Her Standing There, that he had directly taken Chuck Berry's I'm Talking About You.

Later when he was prompted on why the Sergeant Pepper cover did not include Presley, he said, "Elvis was too important and too far above the rest even to mention... so we didn't put him on the list because he was more than merely a... pop singer, he was Elvis the King."

As a fan of Little Richard, McCartney said he loved to impersonate him and that he used his falsetto vocalisations in his own singing. Later, in 1971, McCartney bought the publishing rights to Buddy Holly's entire catalogue.

Having learned music by ear and largely by teaching himself, he said, "I prefer to think of my approach to music as... rather like the primitive cave artists, who drew without training."

Sometimes through boredom and sometimes because of the challenges of members of the Beatles' line-up, McCartney continued to learn new instruments throughout his career. He mastered bass guitar, acoustic guitar, electric guitar, keyboards, piano, and drums, as well as singing throughout his musical life.

"Paul is one of the most innovative bass players... half the stuff that's going on now is directly ripped off from his Beatles period... He's an egomaniac about everything else, but his bass playing he'd always been a bit coy about."

– Lennon, Playboy magazine, January 1981

The Silver Beatles on stage in 1960 in Liverpool, England

Playing with a plectrum, McCartney does not employ other techniques, although on occasions he plays with his fingers. Inspired by Motown, he has been said to like to play bass more 'sensitively'. Beatles biographers and writers have said his playing of the bass matured on the album Rubber Soul.

In 1963, McCartney was interviewed by actress and journalist Jane Asher and began a five-year relationship with her. They were engaged when she discovered McCartney in bed with American scriptwriter Francie Schwartz and ended the relationship.

He also played all the instruments he had mastered on various Beatles tracks, along with an extensive list of vocals for the band's tracks. He was not afraid to experiment and try out new formats, instruments and along the way discovered tape looping as a technique.

At the height of The Beatles fame, in 1969, McCartney met and married an American photographer, musician, and animal rights activist, Linda. He adopted her daughter Heather Louise, from her first marriage to Joseph Melville See. The McCartneys had three children: Mary Anna, Stella Nina, and James Louis.

After The Beatles disbanded in 1970, McCartney had a rocky, brotherly, competitive relationship with Lennon. After a brief reconciliation in 1974, McCartney and Lennon played together, although they apparently avoided talk about their musical careers, preferring to discuss their home and personal lives instead.

In 1976, they (humorously perhaps) considered reforming briefly while they were together watching Saturday Night Live in Lennon's New York City home, where one of the hosts offered a sum of $3000 to reunite the band. Sadly, this would be the last occasion McCartney would see Lennon.

Paul McCartney, the last of the Beatles to marry, poses with his bride Linda Eastman after their wedding at Marylebone Register Office

British actress Jane Asher, girlfriend Paul McCartney, taken in 1965

Paul McCartney (center) holds up the hands of the late John Lennon's
son Sean Lennon (left) and his wife Yoko Ono (right)

Describing the news of Lennon's death, he recalled the press' reaction to his response to Lennon's death, explaining, "When John was killed somebody stuck a microphone at me and said: 'What do you think about it?' I said, 'It's a dra-a-ag' and meant it with every inch of melancholy I could muster. When you put that in print it says, 'McCartney in London today when asked for a comment on his dead friend said, "It's a drag".' It seemed a very flippant comment to make."

He also talked of his conversations with Ono, "I talked to Yoko the day after he was killed, and the first thing she said was, 'John was really fond of you.' The last telephone conversation I had with him we were still the best of mates. He was always a very warm guy, John. His bluff was all on the surface. He used to take his glasses down, those granny glasses, and say, 'it's only me.' They were like a wall you know? A shield. Those are the moments I treasure."

Later, in 1983, he said, "I would not have been as typically human and standoffish as I was if I knew John was going to die. I would have made more of an effort to try and get behind his 'mask' and have a better relationship with him."

"John is kinda like a constant... always there in my being... in my soul, so I always think of him."

– *Paul McCartney, interview with Guitar World, 2000*

Paul McCartney and his wife Linda recording a Wings song, circa 1976

Paul McCartney, still going strong, playing at the Grammy Awards in 2012

Like Lennon, McCartney himself had pursued a solo career. It was somewhat overshadowed by Lennon's earlier solo success and later his death. Regardless, his first solo release, self-titled McCartney went to Number One in the US. He collaborated with his wife Linda, forming the group Wings with her and singer-songwriter Denny Laine. The band would achieve musical heights again with their second album Red Rose Speedway, securing Number One in the US and top five in the UK.

In March 1973, Wings achieved their first US number-one single, 'My Love', included on their second LP, Red Rose Speedway, a US number one and UK top five. The album Band on the Run followed with more success, and went on to be the first of seven platinum Wings albums.

McCartney continued with his musical career long after The Beatles, and continues to today, collaborating with various artists, and continuing to experiment with music. He and Starr also later promoted The Beatles: Rock Band and he has since performed Beatles numbers at various concerts.

Following Linda's death from breast cancer in 1998, McCartney has since married and divorced Heather Mills and married again in 2011 to Nancy Shevell.

McCartney remains a big player in the music industry, having been described by the Guinness World Records as the "most successful composer and recording artist of all time," holding an astonishing 60 gold discs, with sales of over 100 million albums and 100 million singles.

McCartney wrote, or co-wrote, 32 Number One songs on the Billboard Hot 100.

Over 2,200 artists have covered his song Yesterday, which is more than any other song in history. He was inducted into the Rock and Roll Hall of Fame as a solo artist in 1999.

McCartney playing with Wings in 1973

Paul McCartney performs
onstage during the Queen's
Diamond Jubilee Concert at
Buckingham Palace in London
on June 4th, 2012

George Harrison

The youngest of four children, George Harrison was born on February 25th, 1943 to Louise and Harold in Liverpool. Harrison lived his early childhood in a terraced house at 12 Arnold Grove, Wavertree. With only a humble income, the family home had an outdoor toilet and was heated by a single coal fire. His mother was a shop assistant and his father a bus conductor.

Six years later, the family was offered government housing and accepted, moving in to 25 Upton Green, Speke. Aged five, he attended Dovedale Primary School and went on to pass his exams and like McCartney, went to the esteemed Liverpool Institute. Harrison struggled academically and left without any qualifications.

As a young man, he wore tight jeans and had long hair. Harrison later said that as a young child, he heard Presley's Heartbreak Hotel and was inspired to play rock and roll. "I was totally into guitars."

Harrison was known to sit in the back of the classroom drawing guitars and his mother bought him a cheap acoustic guitar, which he soon after broke. Harrison's future wife, Pattie Boyd would describe his parents as supportive of his musical direction, "All she wanted for her children is that they should be happy, and she recognized that nothing made George quite as happy as making music."

Harrison was a young fan of George Formby, Cab Calloway, Django Reinhardt, Hoagy Carmichael, and Big Bill Broonzy. While not as keen on his musical obsession as his mother, Harrison's father was also supportive and bought him another guitar. While at the Institute, Harrison formed a skiffle group called the Rebels. And, after meeting McCartney on the bus ride, he bonded with him over their musical influences. Like Lennon and McCartney's complex relationship, Harrison and McCartney had their ups and downs to come.

1957 Gretsch Duo Jet guitar fitted with a Bigsby Vibrato owned by George Harrison and used in the early years with The Beatles

George Harrison developed a love of music from an early age, this picture was taken in 1954

Harrison taking a break from playing at the Cavern, Liverpool, 1960

On McCartney, Harrison said, "Paul would always help along when you'd done his ten songs—then when he got 'round to doing one of my songs, he would help. It was silly. It was very selfish, actually... There were a lot of tracks, though, where I played bass... because what Paul would do—if he'd written a song, he'd learn all the parts for Paul and then come in the studio and say (sometimes he was very difficult): 'Do this.' He'd never give you the opportunity to come out with something."

On Harrison's death, McCartney said of him, that he was "a lovely guy and a very brave man who had a wonderful sense of humor."

"We grew up together and we just had so many beautiful times together – that's what I am going to remember. I'll always love him, he's my baby brother."

After Harrison auditioned for the Quarrymen, where he reportedly played Guitar Boogie Shuffle, Lennon thought he was too young. It was McCartney who persisted on Harrison's behalf, organizing a second meeting. After he began hanging out with the group, Harrison would play guitar as needed and by the time he turned 15, he was a part of the band.

Harrison left school at 16 and worked as an apprentice electrician for a few months, and while the Quarrymen went quiet for a while, Harrison joined a group called the Les Stewart Quartet. When this group secured a residency at a coffee club in 1959, and two of the group did not show up to play, Lennon and McCartney were called in to fill in and for the gig, used the Quarrymen name.

In 1960, the group was offered a contract to play The Cavern Club and after they had renamed the band to become The Beatles, Harrison was a part of the band who went on to fulfill the residency also in Hamburg.

A studio shot of George from 1962

Harrison honed his musical skills during the residency and took lessons from Tony Sheridan. Later becoming known as the 'quiet Beatle', Harrison focused his energy on guitar playing and led the more subtle lead guitar work that is recognized as being quite different from the attention-seeking, long solo electric guitar work that became popular. As the Rolling Stone magazine founder, Iann Wenner said, "Harrison was a guitarist who was never showy but who had an innate, eloquent melodic sense. He played exquisitely in the service of the song". In fact, many quickly identified that Harrison brought a country feel to the band, being clearly influenced by his music heroes Chet Atkins and Carl Perkins.

When Harrison joined the group, he traded his acoustic for an electric guitar, the Höfner Club 40 model. Harrison also played a variety of Gretch and much later a Rickenbacker 360/12, a 12-string he was given around the time the band recorded A Hard Day's Night, which of course helped Rickenbacker to soar in popularity.

Harrison records on a Rickenbacker electric guitar in the studio in circa 1965

It was during the filming of A Hard Day's Night, The Beatles first movie, that Harrison met Pattie Boyd, who was a model and was cast as a schoolgirl fan. She initially declined Harrison's advances, out of faithfulness to her then fiancé, a photographer. Boyd later said Harrison had asked her, "Will you marry me? Well, if you won't marry me, will you have dinner with me tonight?" When Boyd was asked back to film more footage for the movie, Harrison again asked her out and having ended her relationship with her fiancée, she this time accepted Harrison's invitation. Harrison and Boyd lived together before marrying in 1966 at a registry office in Surrey and then honeymooned in the South of France.

In 1965, Harrison used his first Fender Stratocaster in Rubber Soul and later painted it with psychedelic designs. On this album, Harrison encouraged his bandmates to lean towards folk rock, which was inspired by his love of Bob Dylan and the group the Byrds.

Boyd's interest in Eastern mysticism and spirituality led to Harrison's and the band's introduction to an Indian mystic in London.

Harrison in the studio in 1964

Harrison developed a strong interest in Eastern philosophy, choosing Eastern gurus and religious leaders for the Sergeant Pepper's cover and played sitar and tambura on the track Within You Without You. He also played swarmandal on Strawberry Fields Forever. Harrison began to explore Hinduism and meditation and bonded with Bob Dylan and his band, finding their shared music making and communal approach refreshing. Harrison also showed a curiosity for the Hare Krishna movement, and introduced Indian culture and mysticism to his bandmates and to their Western fans.

George Harrison and his wife, Pattie Boyd

In 1969, Harrison grew tired of McCartney's dominance and Lennon's disengagement within the band and left in January. Persuaded to come back, he returned 12 days later.

He also gained notoriety for his work on slide guitar, when he soloed on Lennon's How Do You Sleep? Lennon said, "That's the best he's ever f***** played in his life."

During the last Beatles album recording, Abbey Road, Harrison composed Here Comes the Sun and Something, which Frank Sinatra recorded himself and later claimed it, "the greatest love song of the past fifty years." Lennon considered it the best song on the album.

Harrison received critical acclaim and was awarded the Ivor Novello award for Something, which was described by author Kenneth Womack, "'Something' meanders toward the most unforgettable of Harrison's guitar solos, the song's greatest lyrical feature—even more lyrical, interestingly enough, than the lyrics themselves. A masterpiece in simplicity, [it] reaches toward the sublime."

Along with penning the Beatle's songs Taxman, Within You Without You, While My Guitar Gently Weeps, Here Comes the Sun, For You Blue, and Something, Harrison also released several best-selling singles and albums as a solo performer.

In 1988, Harrison co-founded the enormously popular supergroup the Traveling Wilburys. Rolling Stone magazine ranked him number 11 in their 100 Greatest Guitarists of All Time.

Top; George Harrison performing at The Cow Palace in Daly City, California on November 7th, 1974

Above; George sits for a photo during a party, 1971

Harrison tunes his Gretsch 6122 Country Gentleman guitar whilst recording She Loves You in 1963

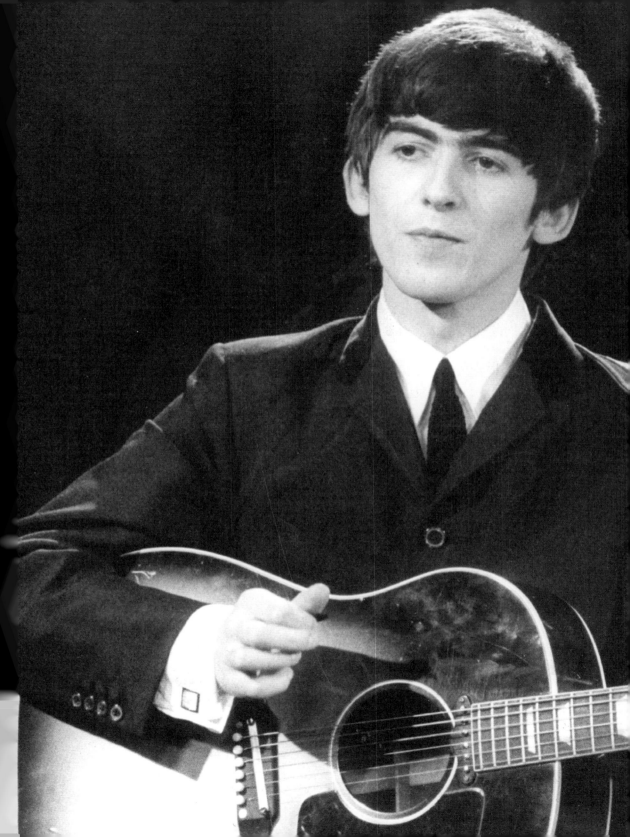

After divorcing Boyd in 1977, Harrison married Olivia Trinidad Arias, a British-Mexican author, film producer, in 1978, and had a son Dhani with her.

That same year, he discovered a cancerous lump. He said, "I got it purely from smoking. I gave up cigarettes many years ago, but had started again for a while and then stopped in 1997. Luckily for me they found that this nodule was more of a warning than anything else.

"It reminds you that anything can happen."

In 1999, Harrison's second wife saved his life by striking an intruder in their family home with a poker and a lamp. The intruder, 36-year-old Michael Abram had broken into their home and started attacking Harrison with a kitchen knife. Harrison had suffered 40 stab wounds, a punctured lung, and head injuries from the attack.

Harrison displayed his typical humor, issuing a statement after release from the hospital which stated that his assailant, "wasn't a burglar, and he certainly wasn't auditioning for the Traveling Wilburys."

Later, in May 2001, Harrison announced he had undergone an operation to remove cancer from one of his lungs. A month later, it was reported that he was treated for a brain tumor at a clinic in Switzerland.

Starr said that when he visited him in Switzerland, he had to cut his stay short to travel to Los Angeles because his daughter was undergoing emergency brain surgery, Harrison quipped, "Do you want me to come with you?"

Then, in November, Harrison had radiotherapy for lung cancer that had spread to his brain.

Sadly, the quiet Beatle passed away on November 29th, 2001, at 58, from lung cancer. The spiritual man that Harrison was, his ashes were scattered in Varanasi, India, in the Ganges, Saraswati, and Yamuna Rivers by his close family in a private ceremony according to Hindu tradition.

Harrison performing for TV cameras in 1963

"George was a giant, a great, great soul, with all of the humanity, all of the wit and humor, all the wisdom, the spirituality, the common sense of a man and compassion for people. The world is a profoundly emptier place without him."

– *Bob Dylan*

"You always knew where you stood with George, he was totally honest. I feel blessed to have been so close to him. He was a great friend. Some of the happiest days of my life were spent in the studio with George."

– *Jeff Lynne*

In a statement to the press and public, his family said, "He left this world as he lived in it, conscious of God, fearless of death, and at peace, surrounded by family and friends.

'He often said, 'Everything else can wait but the search for God cannot wait, and love one another'.'"

Harrison's death caused an outpouring of grief and sadness around the world. As the youngest Beatle, it shocked many when he became ill and finally passed. Fans laid tributes in London outside the Abbey Road studios, his home, and the Cavern Club in Liverpool. In the US, fans gathered at Strawberry Fields to remember him.

Starr told the press, "We will miss George for his sense of love, his sense of music and his sense of laughter." And Lennon's widow, Ono, said: "My deep love and concern goes to Olivia and Dhani."

George Harrison with his wife Olivia Harrison at Caprice Restaurant on February 5th, 1990 in London.

Harrison at a fundraiser in 1999

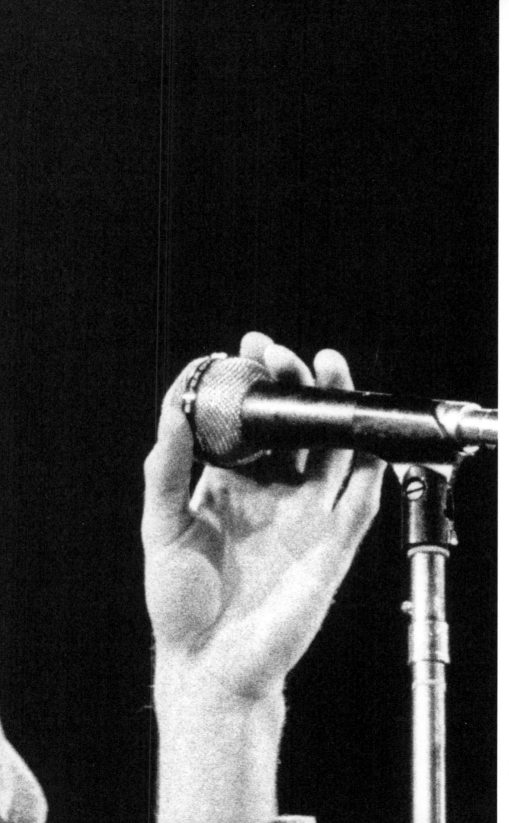

Harrison performing
live in 1974

*George Harrison at the Billboard
Music Awards, Las Vegas, 2000*

Queen Elizabeth announced she was "very sad to hear of the death of George Harrison". Then-Prime Minister Tony Blair said, "People of my generation grew up with The Beatles, and they were the background to our lives."

According to reports, his will consisted of an estate of almost £100 million. His son completed his last album and posthumously released it, titled Brainwashed in 2002. In the album's liner notes is a quotation from the Bhagavad Gita: "There never was a time when you or I did not exist. Nor will there be any future when we shall cease to be."

Two singles from the album reached the charts and in 2004, Marwa Blues from the record received a Grammy Award for Best Pop Instrumental Performance, and Any Road was nominated for Best Male Pop Vocal Performance.

"I am devastated and very, very sad, ... We knew he'd been ill for a long time. He was a lovely guy and a very brave man and had a wonderful sense of humor. He is really just my baby brother."

"Something like George passing, it makes you think, `God, things are so impermanent: suddenly there's this little friend of mine, he used to get on the bus, and now he's passed away.' There's that whole lifetime of a friendship that physically has ended, not emotionally."

– *Paul McCartney*

George Harrison poses for a portrait with Indian sitar virtuoso Ravi Shankar in 1975

*George writing new
material in 1971*

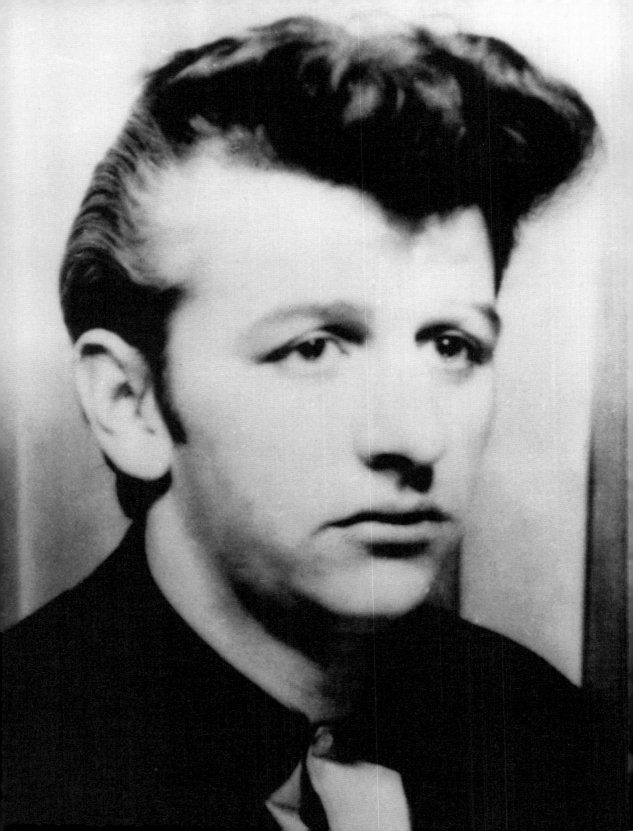

Ringo Starr

Ringo Starr, not his real name, was born Richard Starkey on July 7th, 1940. Delivered at home, 9 Madryn Street, Dingle in Liverpool, Starr was the son of Elsie and Richard, a confectioner. His parents broke up when he was three years old. His mother later remarried and Starr's stepfather encouraged his interest in music. A sickly child, Starr suffered appendicitis with complications when he was just six years of age, causing him to fall into a coma.

Attending a Church of England primary school in High Park Street, close to his home in Admiral Grove, Starr then later went to Dingle Vale Secondary Modern School where he showed an aptitude for art and drama as well as practical subjects including mechanics.

At the age of 13, Starr had chronic pleurisy, inflammation of the lining of the lungs, which meant he had to be admitted to a sanatorium for two years. He did not return to school following this and fell behind in his academic education.

Three poses by Ringo Starr, drummer with The Beatles, 1963

A pre-Beatles Ringo Starr in 1959

Ringo Starr backstage in 1963

In 1957, following his interest in skiffle, he and his friend Eddie Miles formed the Eddie Clayton Skiffle Group. Two years later, he joined the Raving Texans and began using the stage name 'Ringo Starr' because of the rings he wore, because it sounded 'cowboyish', and because his drum solos were billed as 'Starr Time.'

Starr was performing in Hamburg with the newly renamed band, Rory Storm and the Hurricanes, in 1960 when he met the other members of the 'Fab Four' and recorded with them when backing the Hurricanes' singer Lu Walters.

After Starr filled in for Pete Best on a couple of occasions, he was invited to join the group following Best's departure after their first EMI recording. He first performed live with them in August of 1962, and on his second appearance faced fans of Best's who were outraged at his dismissal. They chanted, 'Pete forever! Ringo never!' Apparently the crowds were so hostile, Harrison was the recipient of a black eye from one of the fans.

After arriving at the studios for the September recording with EMI, Starr said, "I thought, 'That's the end, they're doing a Pete Best on me.'" Martin had asked session drummer Andy White to record, and Starr said, "He [George Martin] thought I was crazy and couldn't play. Because when we were doing 'Please Please Me', I was actually playing the kit and in one hand I had a tambourine and a maracas in the other, because I was trying to play the percussion and the drums at the same time, because we were just a four piece band."

The Beatles performing 'Paperback Writer' &
'Rain', on TV show Top of the Pops

Ringo playing in a Pierre Cardin suit in 1963

Starr, in fact, became a very popular drummer, receiving critical acclaim and fellow musician's praise for his creative drumming. He also provided vocal contributions to The Beatles tracks, although his limited range meant Lennon and McCartney would write lyrics and melody especially for him.

Starr often inspired The Beatles with his unique turns of phrase, such as 'a hard day's night' and 'tomorrow never knows'. The band dubbed them 'Ringoisms' and turned them into song lyrics.

McCartney said, "Ringo would do these little malapropisms, he would say things slightly wrong, like people do, but his were always wonderful, very lyrical... they were sort of magic."

In 1964, Starr was at a photoshoot and became very ill with 102-degree fever and tonsillitis and was rushed to hospital. After Starr needed recuperation time, Epstein arranged for drummers to fill in on his behalf. On his return, Epstein gave Starr a check and a gold Eterna-matic wristwatch inscribed: "From The Beatles and Brian Epstein to Jimmy – with appreciation and gratitude." Starr confessed much later he was actually very worried they would replace him altogether.

The Beatles pose for promotional material in 1963

Ringo Starr performing live onstage at Circus-Krone-Bau on final German tour, 24th June 1966

In 1965, Starr married Maureen Cox, who he had met while playing The Cavern Club. Cox was a trainee hairdresser and went on to have three children with Starr before divorcing him in 1975.

Like Harrison, Starr got fed up with the tension in the band and, while waiting to contribute to the recording session for the White Album, left the band. Harrison and McCartney had argued over McCartney's criticizing Starr's drumming for Back in the U.S.S.R. After taking two weeks out on Peter Seller's yacht, he wrote the song Octopus' Garden and returned to find flowers placed on his drum kit.

While generally popular in the band and with fans and industry folk alike, Starr also had rocky relationship moments with McCartney.

Starr said McCartney was "pleasantly insincere." He also commented, "Paul is the greatest bass player in the world. But he is also very determined ... [to] get his own way ... [thus] musical disagreements inevitably arose from time to time."

Peter Brown said, "it was a poorly kept secret among Beatle intimates that after Ringo left the studio Paul would often dub in the drum tracks himself ... [Starr] would pretend not to notice." Generally, though, they got along, and had vacationed together, and they later collaborated together on albums in the 70s, 80s, and 90s.

Ringo Star with girlfriend Maureen Cox, 1964

Starr went on to write Taking a Trip to Carolina on the second CD of Let It Be... Naked, and received joint songwriting credits for a string of Beatles songs.

In 2011, Rolling Stone readers picked Starr as the fifth-best drummer of all-time. Starr said, "Whenever I hear another drummer I know I'm no good. I'm no good on the technical things... I'm your basic offbeat drummer with funny fills. The fills were funny because I'm really left-handed playing a right-handed kit. I can't roll around the drums because of that."

However, contrary to what Starr originally assumed Martin thought of his skills, Martin said, "Ringo hit good and hard and used the tom-tom well, even though he couldn't do a roll to save his life...

"He's got tremendous feel. He always helped us to hit the right tempo for a song, and gave it that support – that rock-solid back-beat – that made the recording of all The Beatles' songs that much easier."

Phil Collins, singer and drummer of Genesis, said, "Starr is vastly underrated. The drum fills on the song 'A Day in the Life' are very complex things. You could take a great drummer today and say, 'I want it like that.' He wouldn't know what to do."

Lennon, in 1980, said of Starr, "Ringo was a star in his own right in Liverpool before we even met. He was a professional drummer who sang and performed and had Ringo Starr-time and he was in one of the top groups in Britain but especially in Liverpool before we even had a drummer. So Ringo's talent would have come out one way or the other as something or other. I don't know what he would have ended up as, but whatever that spark is in Ringo that we all know but can't put our finger on — whether it is acting, drumming, or singing I don't know – there is something in him that is projectable and he would have surfaced with or without The Beatles. Ringo is a damn good drummer."

Ringo playing the drums in the recording studio during sessions for B.B. King In London

Paul McCartney (right) and Ringo Starr (left) introduce the new video game 'The Beatles: Rock Band' at the Microsoft XBox 360 E3 2009 gaming expo new conference on June 1, 2009

He is also is the most documented and critically acclaimed actor among The Beatles, and achieved solo musical success with several singles and albums. Interestingly, given his acting talents, he has also hosted TV shows, narrated the first two series of Thomas the Tank Engine & Friends and played 'Mr. Conductor' during the first season of another children's television series, Shining Time Station. Starr has toured with the Ringo Starr & His All-Starr Band since 1989.

In 1980, Starr met actress Barbara Bach on the set of the film Caveman, who was most famous for her role as Major Anya Amasova (female lead and main 'Bond girl') in The Spy Who Loved Me. They married the following year and are still married today.

On meeting Starr, Bach said, "I was never that much of a Beatles fan, which made it easier. I just treated him like anyone else. As time went on, however, I was touched by his generosity. He is so patient and understanding. Let me give you an example. Ritchie can't swim, but there's a scene where he has to rescue me from a river. Carl said they could use a stunt man, but it'd be better if Ritchie jumped in. So he jumps. By the time he reaches me, he's headed for the bottom. And when we get to the rock I'm literally pushing him up."

"I don't think I could have named five of their songs a year ago. I was never really into music, though I am now – up to my ears. I'm surrounded by it because Richard is making another album."

Top: Ringo Starr models as the Fat Controller with train characters from the TV series, Thomas the Tank Engine, which he narrated, 1985

Above: Ringo Starr taping the TV show Shining Time Station, 1989

Ringo Starr and His All-Starr Band in concert at Jones Beach Theater on June 22, 1989 in Wantagh, New York

Ringo Starr performs a solo show live at the Hordern Pavilion on February 13th, 2013 in Sydney, Australia

Although happily married, they both struggled with alcoholism and in 1988, a friend said of their dependency, "Their biggest problem was alcohol. They've both been drinking heavily every day for years. Ringo and Barbara are also cocaine users. Ringo had been snorting up to a gram of coke a day and Barbara said she'd been using about half a gram daily. In addition, Ringo has a history of free basing (smoking cocaine). He also smoked marijuana every day and used hallucinogenics, mushrooms, and downers. Ringo said that since they'd been married virtually all they've done is sit in a room and use drugs. Barbara revealed that it was the number one priority in their lives – more important than family, more important than each other, more important than anything. Both said they were convinced they were going to die unless they got help."

At this point they were consuming so much alcohol they both suffered blackouts and memory loss. One day Starr received the shock he needed to clean up.

He said, "I trashed Barbara so bad I thought she was dead. They just found her covered in blood and I'd beaten her up and I'd no idea…"

Starr checked the couple into a rehabilitation clinic, the Sierra Tucson Rehabilitation Clinic where Bach apparently said, "Please, if you don't help us we're going to die."

They have both been free from drugs and alcohol since. In 1991, with help from Pattie Boyd, Barbara set up a free clinic for addicts called SHARP (Self Help Addiction Recovery Programme) in London.

Starr has been credited with influencing modern drumming, introducing tuning the drums lower, using muffling devices on tonal rings, and making the drums highly visible. He has inspired drummers such as Steve Gorman of the Black Crowes, Don Henley of The Eagles, Dave Grohl of Nirvana, and many more.

Ringo still going strong in 2001

Ringo Starr and His All-Starr Band perform live during a concert at the Congress Center on June 29th, 2011 in Prague, Czech Republic

Left to right: Paul McCartney, George Harrison, Ringo Starr, and John
Lennon dash down a street in the 1964 Beatles film A Hard Day's Night

The Beatles at the Movies

While The Beatles were more famous for their music than their movies, they received praise and positivity for the majority of their five films. Naturally, for each film there was an accompanying soundtrack and title song to match.

Mirroring their light-hearted and comic approach to the media furore over their early success and Beatlemania, their first film was the comedy A Hard Day's Night. Filmed and released in 1964, at the height of Beatlemania, it was shot for United Artists, in black and white in just under seven weeks. Well received by critics and popular with the band's fans, the film was loosely based on their chaotic touring and lifestyle as the famous Beatles.

"We went to do a job, and we'd worked all day and we happened to work all night. I came up still thinking it was day I suppose, and I said, 'It's been a hard day...' and I looked around and saw it was dark so I said, '...night!' So we came to A Hard Day's Night."
– *Ringo Starr, in an interview with DJ Dave Hull in 1964*

"The title was Ringo's. We'd almost finished making the film, and this fun bit arrived that we'd not known about before, which was naming the film. So we were sitting around at Twickenham studios having a little brain-storming session... and we said, 'Well, there was something Ringo said the other day.' Ringo would do these little malapropisms, he would say things slightly wrong, like people do, but his were always wonderful, very lyrical... they were sort of magic even though he was just getting it wrong. And he said after a concert, 'Phew, it's been a hard day's night.'"

– *McCartney, in a 1994 interview for The Beatles Anthology*

The Beatles, (top to bottom) Ringo Starr, George Harrison, John Lennon, and Paul McCartney, all piled on top of a sled in the snow during the making of their second feature film Help!

British film critic Leslie Halliwell gave the movie four out of four stars and said it was a "comic fantasia with music; an enormous commercial success with the director trying every cinematic gag in the book."

In addition to the critical acclaim the film received, Time magazine rated it one of the all-time great 100 films, calling it "One of the smoothest, freshest, funniest films ever made for purposes of exploitation." It was also said to have inspired films, television shows, and music videos of the future.

The movie had been compared to the Marx Brothers in style and was directed by Richard Lester who was well known for his direction of The Goon Show and the film The Running, Jumping and Standing Still Film, with Peter Sellers and Spike Milligan. Lester's comedic direction was a good match for the screenplay, which was written by Alun Owen. The plot focuses on days in the lives of the band members, leading up to their appearance on television, and was described a 'mockumentary'.

Owen was selected to write the screenplay as he was familiar with Liverpudlian humor and conversation, so his dialogue was to The Beatles' liking. The band also knew him from his screenplay No Trams to Lime Street.

McCartney commented, "Alun hung around with us and was careful to try and put words in our mouths that he might've heard us speak, so I thought he did a very good script."

The writer also spent time with the group, who told him their lives were like "a train and a room and a car and a room and a room and a room," which is why McCartney's grandfather in the film refers to this.

George Harrison (left), John Lennon (right), Paul McCartney, and Ringo Starr (background) on set at the Scala Theatre during the filming of A Hard Day's Night

The Beatles stand in a window at Twickenham Film Studios, Middlesex

The Beatles pose for a portrait on the set of their movie
Help! which was released on August 25th, 1965

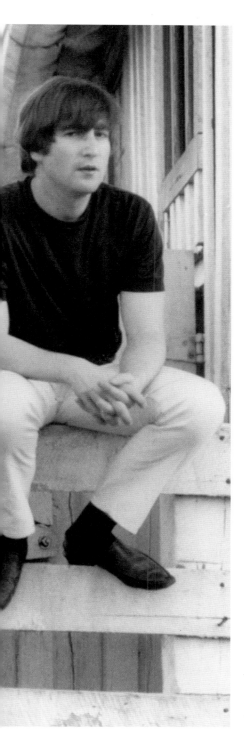

Making light of the band's hectic schedule, he focused on this and centered the plot around how they were trapped in their success and fame. Poking fun at Beatlemania, the main storyline follows The Beatles as they are hassled by their manager, their fans, and McCartney's grandfather, while they travel from Liverpool to London by train to meet their television appearance commitment. On board the train, the group encounters various interruptions and after they are continually disturbed, Harrison moves to the goods van for quiet.

After arriving in London, the group go to a hotel from which they feel they cannot escape. Later, while filming their appearance, Starr leaves unnoticed and has a leisurely time, taking a drink at a pub, riding a bicycle, and after the remaining band members search for him frantically, he ends up arrested and returns to the filming.

Making fun of themselves, The Beatles have a number of scenes in the movie that showcase the self-deprecating sense of humor they possessed.

In one scene, a fan recognizes Lennon, but says "you are..." The fan and Lennon end up agreeing that Lennon doesn't "look like him at all" and Lennon says to himself that "she looks more like him than I do."

In another, Ringo is asked if he's a Mod or a Rocker, "Uh, no, I'm a mocker." There is also an amusing scene where their television show features photos of beetles (insects) on the wall. Owen's screenplay was nominated for an Oscar.

Filmed with a low budget (even for its time), totaling just £200,000, the UA executives were more interested in the soundtrack that would accompany the movie. As Bud Ornstein, the European head of production for United Artists, said: "Our record division wants to get the soundtrack album to distribute in the States, and what we lose on the film we'll get back on this disc."

For its release in the States, the director Lester was asked to dub the voices of the group with mid-Atlantic accents. McCartney angrily replied, "Look, if we can understand a f****** cowboy talking Texan, they can understand us talking Liverpool."

Ringo Starr performing onstage, on the set of 'A Hard Day's Night' at the Scala Theatre, playing Ludwig drum kit

In addition to the 'Fab Four' as the main actors and characters in the film, A Hard Day's Night also featured Epstein, who went unaccredited, as well as Irish actor Wilfrid Brambell, who played McCartney's fictional grandfather John McCartney. Brambell was famous to British audiences, being one of the stars of the British sitcom Steptoe and Son. Because Brambell's character in the sitcom was referred to as a 'dirty old man', The Beatles' film makes a number of references to him being clean.

Genesis musician, Phil Collins, also appears unaccredited in the movie – as a boy in the concert audience.

Premiering in July of 1964, the film set a new record at the London Pavilion, taking in over £13,800 ($20,000) in the first week. It went on to enjoy immense popularity with audiences and critics. By 1971, the film had earned an estimated £7.5 million ($11 million) worldwide.

New Yorker critic Brendan Gill wrote: "Though I don't pretend to understand what makes these four rather odd-looking boys so fascinating to so many scores of millions of people, I admit that I feel a certain mindless joy stealing over me as they caper about, uttering sounds."

Another critic, Roger Ebert, described the film as "one of the great life-affirming landmarks of the movies." Indeed, it was nominated for two Academy Awards; for Best Screenplay (Alun Owen), and Best Score (Adaptation) (George Martin).

The soundtrack followed four days after the premiere, also to a rapturous reception.

The Beatles (left to right) Ringo Starr, John Lennon, and George Harrison pose for a photo with a local marching band in March 1965 in Obertauern, Austria while filming Help!

Paul McCartney poses in the snow for the film Help!

The following year, in 1965 Lester directed the group again in the film Help! Shot in exotic locations around Europe, the movie was another spoof, this time filmed in color. A comedy adventure, the band comes up against an evil cult, where a woman is about to be sacrificed.

"We showed up a bit stoned, smiled a lot and hoped we'd get through it. We giggled a lot. I remember one time at Cliveden (Lord Astor's place, where the Christine Keeler/Profumo scandal went on); we were filming the Buckingham Palace scene where we were all supposed to have our hands up. It was after lunch, which was fatal because someone might have brought out a glass of wine as well. We were all a bit merry and all had our backs to the camera and the giggles set in. All we had to do was turn around and look amazed, or something. But every time we'd turn round to the camera there were tears streaming down our faces. It's OK to get the giggles anywhere else but in films, because the technicians get pissed off with you. They think, 'They're not very professional.' Then you start thinking, 'This isn't very professional – but we're having a great laugh.'"

– Paul McCartney

"The movie was out of our control. With A Hard Day's Night, we had a lot of input, and it was semi-realistic. But with Help!, Dick Lester didn't tell us what it was all about."

– John Lennon on filming Help!

The woman to be sacrificed is not wearing the sacrificial ring, which had been secretly sent to Starr by the woman's sister. To retrieve the ring, the cult members seek out The Beatles and attempt to steal the ring. Starr then discovers that he will be sacrificed if he does not return the ring, and goes on to discover the ring cannot be removed from his finger.

The Beatles pose for a portrait in front of water with wind blown hair on the set of the Movie Help!

The rest of the film sees Starr and the band making various attempts at removing the ring, through a jeweler and a mad scientist. Much silliness follows, including the magical shrinking of Starr, attempts on the band's lives, and crazy escape acts. The group said the film was inspired by the Marx Brothers' Duck Soup and sent up the Bond film franchise.

Fitting with the humor popular in the mid-60s, The Goon Show was a clear influence on the band's offbeat humor. Critical acclaim did not follow this film, but audiences were kinder.

Film critic Leslie Halliwell described it as an, "[e]xhausting attempt to outdo A Hard Day's Night in lunatic frenzy, which goes to show that some talents work best on low budgets. The humor is a frantic cross between Hellzapoppin', The Goons, Goofy, Mr. Magoo, and the shade of Monty Python to come. It looks good but becomes too tiresome to entertain."

A gentler review came from Allmovie's Ronnie D. Lankford, Jr. who wrote Help! was "... a forerunner to music videos. ... Lester seemed to find the right tone for Help!, creating an enjoyable portrait of The Beatles and never allowing the film to take itself too seriously. His style would later be co-opted by Bob Rafaelson [sic] for the Monkees' television series in the '60s and has continued to influence rock musicals like Spice World in 1998."

Lennon, Paul McCartney, Ringo Starr, and George Harrison pose for a photo in the snow in March 1965

The Beatles (left to right) Ringo Starr, Paul McCartney, George Harrison, and John Lennon in March 1965 while filming Help!

After a two-year break from movies, McCartney came up with the idea to film Magical Mystery Tour, after he returned from a trip to the States in the spring of 1967. Inspired by press coverage McCartney saw on Ken Kesey's Merry Pranksters' LSD-fueled American bus odyssey, McCartney thought it would work well with the very English working class tradition of charabanc mystery tours. These tours were chaperoned bus rides for children through the English countryside, with an unknown destination.

"I'm not sure whose idea Magical Mystery Tour was. It could have been mine, but I'm not sure whether I want to take the blame for it! We were all in on it — but a lot of the material at that time could have been my idea."

– McCartney, after the band members said it was his concept

Unscripted, the film was shot using sketches and ideas. It was filmed over a two-week period, although editing took 11 weeks. Gathering a group of people as cast, it was made up as it was filmed. The bus tour involved strange happenings conjured up from magicians, an impromptu race, and a visit to an Army recruitment office.

 Lennon said in an interview much later, "We knew most of the scenes we wanted to include, but we bent our ideas to fit the people concerned, once we got to know our cast. If somebody wanted to do something we hadn't planned, they went ahead. If it worked, we kept it in."

Paul McCartney on the set of Magical Mystery Tour

Magical Mystery Tour cast, 1967

The film aired on BBC1 on Boxing Day, December 26th, 1967. Audiences and critics alike received it poorly. In addition to interrupting the usual Boxing Day family viewing, the film was criticized for being shot in color when only a small audience of viewers in the UK had color receivers at this time.

Martin said: "When it came out originally on British television, it was a color film shown in black and white, because they didn't have color on BBC1 in those days. It looked awful and was a disaster." It was aired in color on BBC2 a few days later, although only around 200,000 viewers had receivers.

McCartney later said, "We don't say it was a good film. It was our first attempt. If we goofed, then we goofed. It was a challenge and it didn't come off. We'll know better next time."

"I mean, you couldn't call the Queen's speech a gas, either, could you?"

Much later, McCartney again spoke of the film, "Looking back on it, I thought it was all right. I think we were quite pleased with it."

Because of the scathing reviews, it was not released in the US or in theatres at launch. A negative of the film was not archived, so the film had to be restored much later when featured in a BBC documentary.

Film poster for Magical Mystery Tour

John Lennon during filming of Magical Mystery Tour

Left to right; John Lennon, George Harrison, Ringo Starr, Paul McCartney posed, on bus, during filming of Magical Mystery Tour

Ringo Starr (left) and George Harrison pose with a 'Blue Meanie', a character from their animated musical film Yellow Submarine

The animated Yellow Submarine then followed in 1968, although this had little input from The Beatles. Acclaimed for its innovative graphic style and boldness, the film and the soundtrack achieved great success. A fantasy, the animation director, George Dunning, focused the plot on a land called Pepperland, a musical paradise.

The Beatles were said to have been pleased with the result and attended its highly publicized London premiere. In it, a yellow submarine sits on a hill surrounded by blue mountains. Sgt. Pepper's Lonely Hearts Club Band protected the land. When music haters, the Blue Meanies, attack Pepperland the Mayor of the land seeks the help of The Beatles.

They journey to Pepperland in the yellow submarine and return to the previously magical land now a scene of devastation. Singing All You Need is Love, the band restore Pepperland to its original bright, vivid colors and in the end everyone lives happily ever after.

The final scene features the real Beatles filmed with 'real life' evidence of their adventures in Pepperland.

According to reports, it took some convincing to involve The Beatles in another film, following the disastrous Magical Mystery Tour. But an animated film became a convenient way to fulfill their three-film contract to UA.

Creative Director of the film, Heinz Edelmann, introduced a style that differed from the Disney Feature Animations that were popular at the time. The film also included four previously unreleased racks of The Beatles, and an orchestral instrumental score composed and arranged by George Martin.

The animation received positive reviews, with Time magazine claiming, it "turned into a smash hit, delighting adolescents and esthetes alike." It was a box office hit.

Three Beatles; from left to right John Lennon, George Harrison, and Paul McCartney, record voices in a studio for their new cartoon film Yellow Submarine

The Beatles then filmed a documentary over four weeks in 1969, Let it Be.

Intended to be a record of their return to live performances, it ended up being a film of the beginning of their break-up. Showcasing the rehearsals and recordings of songs for the album, Let it Be ended up being an apt title, with the group's last performance being a surprise rooftop gig included in the documentary.

John Lennon, Paul McCartney, George Harrison, and Ringo Starr were awarded a joint Academy Award for Best Original Song Score for the film.

Employing an observer, 'fly on the wall', film perspective, it begins with the band rehearsing on a sound stage at Twickenham Film Studios. During a discussion about the development of songs at this session, the viewer witnesses an awkward exchange between McCartney and Harrison over a guitar riff on Two of Us. Harrison says to McCartney: 'I'll play whatever you want me to play, or I won't play at all if you don't want to me to play. Whatever it is that will please you, I'll do it.'

The film also features Yoko Ono, dancing with Lennon, The Beatles arriving separately at Apple headquarters, and Billy Preston accompanying the band on impromptu renditions of several rock covers.

Cameraman Les Parrott said: "My brief on the first day was to 'shoot The Beatles.' The sound crew instructions were to roll/record from the moment the first Beatle appeared and to record sound all day until the last one left. We had two cameras and just about did the same thing."

Apparently, there was a lot of film edited out from the rough cut of the documentary, in particular of Lennon and Ono together. Writer and director Sir Michael Lindsay-Hogg recalled that the rough cut was about an hour longer than the released version: "There was much more stuff of John and Yoko, and the other three didn't really think that was appropriate because they wanted to make it a 'nicer' movie. They didn't want to have a lot of the dirty laundry, so a lot of it was cut down."

Lennon said of the final film, "the camera work was set up to show Paul and not to show anybody else... the people that cut it, cut it as 'Paul is God' and we're just lyin' around ..."

The Beatles performing their last live public concert on the rooftop of the Apple Organization building for director Michael Lindsey-Hogg's film documentary, Let It Be

The final film of The Beatles, Let it Be, was premiered in New York City in May 1970. The UK premieres followed a week later, although none of The Beatles attended any of these.

The British Press attacked it, with The Sunday Telegraph writing, "it is only incidentally that we glimpse anything about their real characters – the way in which music now seems to be the only unifying force holding them together, and the way Paul McCartney chatters incessantly even when, it seems, none of the others are listening."

Lindsay-Hogg, in an interview with Entertainment Weekly in 2003, recalled reception to the film from the band was "mixed".

In particular, he said Harrison thought "it represented a time in his life when he was unhappy ... It was a time when he very much was trying to get out from under the thumb of Lennon–McCartney."

A fresh-faced George Harrison in 1965

Police struggle to hold back the crowd at the London premiere of The Beatles film Let It Be

The Beatles perform onstage in a still from their movie A
Hard Day's Night which was released in 1964

Drugs and Epstein's Death

After meeting Maharishi Mahesh Yogi through Pattie Boyd, The Beatles traveled to Bangor, India, to join him for a transcendental meditation retreat. Two days later, they returned to the news that their much-loved manager Brian Epstein had died.

His autopsy revealed accidental overdoses of carbitol or Bromoureide, a sedative. It was rumored to have been a suicide, as his personal life and his management of The Beatles (which was due to expire that year) stressed Epstein. However, this was never substantiated and his body was found surrounded by paperwork, as if he were working right up to his death.

Lennon recalled, "'We collapsed. I knew that we were in trouble then. I didn't really have any misconceptions about our ability to do anything other than play music, and I was scared. I thought, 'We've had it now.'"

The Beatles were well known for their experimentation with drugs. Many of their musical innovations were linked with their recreational drug taking. The media and some members of the public were critical of this, claiming they had a role to play in leading the youth.

"I never felt any responsibility, being a so-called idol. It's wrong of people to expect it. What they are doing is putting their responsibilities on us, as Paul said to the newspapers when he admitted taking LSD. If they were worried about him being responsible, they should have been responsible enough and not printed it, if they were genuinely worried about people copying."

– John Lennon, 1967

Inset; Maharishi Mahesh Yogi (center), the Indian mystic who introduced the British pop group to transcendental meditation

The Beatles and their wives at the Rishikesh in India with
the Maharishi Mahesh Yogi, March 1968

Three of the Beatles, Ringo Starr, George Harrison, and John Lennon, in Bangor,
North Wales, having just been informed of the death of their manager Brian Epstein

In The Beatles Anthology book, Lennon was quoted as saying his first encounter with drugs was the use of the stimulant Benzedrine: "The first drugs I ever took, I was still at art school, with the group – we all took it together - was Benzedrine from the inside of an inhaler." The beat poet Royston Ellis reportedly introduced them to Benzedrine one night in Liverpool when the group supported his reading.

Harrison recalled, "Ellis had discovered that if you open a Vick's inhaler you find Benzedrine in it, impregnated into the cardboard divide." Lennon also commented, "everyone thought, 'Wow! What's this?' and talked their mouths off for a night."

Ellis later claimed to have inspired the song Paperback Writer. Lennon also wrote the song Polythene Pam about Ellis' girlfriend Stephanie, he said, "[Polythene Pam] was me, remembering a little event with a woman in Jersey, and a man who was England's answer to Allen Ginsberg, who gave us our first exposure - this is so long - you can't deal with all this. You see, everything triggers amazing memories. I met him when we were on tour and he took me back to his apartment and I had a girl and he had one he wanted me to meet. He said she dressed up in polythene, which she did. She didn't wear jackboots and kilts, I just sort of elaborated. Perverted sex in a polythene bag. Just looking for something to write about."

The Beatles' manager Brian Epstein in a press conference at Americana Hotel, 1966

Left to right; John Lennon, Paul McCartney, and George Harrison of The Beatles perform live on stage circa December 1962, during their final residency at the Star-Club in Hamburg

A few years later, McCartney was taught how to extract the drug from an inhaler by his then fiancée, Jane Asher's, father. Dr Richard Asher also shocked McCartney by writing him a prescription for a nasal inhaler when he was ill and showed him how to use it. "You take off the top and place it on your little finger, like so. Then you take a sniff with each nostril as per normal; then, after you've finished with it, you can unscrew the bottom and eat the Benzedrine."

According to McCartney, he was embarrassed, "We learned about that stuff up in Liverpool but hearing it coming from him was quite strange."

The Beatles' involvement and experimentation with drugs really deepened in Hamburg. It was said they took Preludin, or 'prellies', which were German slimming pills, to keep up with the demanding show schedule, to give them the energy.

"In Hamburg the waiters always had Preludin - and various other pills, but I remember Preludin because it was such a big trip - and they were all taking these pills to keep themselves awake, to work these incredible hours in this all-night place. And so the waiters, when they'd see the musicians falling over with tiredness or with drink, they'd give you the pill. You'd take the pill, you'd be talking, you'd sober up, you could work almost endlessly - until the pill wore off, then you'd have to have another."

– John Lennon

George Harrison of the Beatles appears at a press conference on their final German tour (the Bravo-Beatles-Blitztournee) on June 26th, 1966 in Hamburg, Germany.

George Harrison and Stuart Sutcliffe performing live
onstage at Top Ten Club, 1961

John Lennon (playing his first Rickenbacker 325 guitar), and Paul McCartney perform live onstage in Hamburg, 1962

It was well known that most of the bands performing the circuit were consuming the drugs.

"This was the point of our lives when we found pills, uppers. That's the only way we could continue playing for so long. They were called Preludin, and you could buy them over the counter. We never thought we were doing anything wrong, but we'd get really wired and go on for days. So with beer and Preludin, that's how we survived."

– Ringo Starr

Sutcliffe's fiancée Astrid Kirchherr, also supplied the group with the pills, from her mother's medicine cabinet.

"They were actually pills to make slimming easier for you. We used to take them with a couple of beers. They made you just a little speedy. But you can't compare it to speed from today or cocaine or anything. It's just baby food compared to that."

– Astrid Kirchherr, 1996

Lennon was the keenest of the band to use the drugs, with Best sticking to alcohol and McCartney initially being more shy or sensible with his use. This was then followed by their experimentation with speed.

"The speed thing first came from the gangsters. Looking back, they were probably thirty years old but they seemed fifty... They would send a little tray of schnapps up to the band and say, 'You must do this: Bang bang, ya! Proost!' Down in one go. The little ritual. So you'd do that, because these were the owners. They made a bit of fun of us but we played along and let them because we weren't great heroes, we needed their protection and this was life or death country. There were gas guns and murderers amongst us, so you weren't messing around here. They made fun of us because our name, The Beatles, sounded very like the German 'Peedles' which means 'little willies'. 'Oh, zee Peedles! Ha ha ha!' They loved that. It appealed directly to the German sense of humor, that did. So we'd let it be a joke, and we'd drink the schnapps and they'd occasionally send up pills, prellies, Preludin, and say, 'Take one of these.'"

"I knew that was dodgy. I sensed that you could get a little too wired on stuff like that. I went along with it the first couple of times, but eventually we'd be sitting there rapping and rapping, drinking and drinking, and going faster and faster, and I remember John turning round to me and saying, 'What are you on, man? What are you on?' I said, 'Nothin'! 'S great, though, isn't it!' Because I'd just get buoyed up by their conversation. They'd be on the prellies and I would have decided I didn't really need one, I was so wired anyway. Or I'd maybe have one pill, while the guys, John particularly, would have four or five during the course of an evening and get totally wired. I always felt I could have one and get as wired as they got just on the conversation. So you'd find me up just as late as all of them, but without the aid of the prellies. This was good because it meant I didn't have to get into sleeping tablets. I tried all of that but I didn't like sleeping tablets, it was too heavy a sleep. I'd wake up at night and reach for a glass of water and knock it over. So I suppose I was a little bit more sensible than some of the other guys in rock 'n' roll at that time. Something to do with my Liverpool upbringing made me exercise caution."

– *Paul McCartney*

The Beatles and Gene Vincent feeling the effects of Preludin in Hamburg, 1962

The Beatles performing on stage at the Star Club,
Hamburg, 1962

*George Harrison smokes a cigarette
backstage with John Lennon, 1963*

In 1960, The Beatles were offered cannabis in Hamburg, but were underwhelmed by the drug.

"We first got marijuana from an older drummer with another group in Liverpool. We didn't actually try it until after we'd been to Hamburg. I remember we smoked it in the band room in a gig in Southport and we all learnt to do the Twist that night, which was popular at the time. We were all seeing if we could do it. Everybody was saying, 'This stuff isn't doing anything.' It was like that old joke where a party is going on and two hippies are up floating on the ceiling, and one is saying to the other, 'This stuff doesn't work, man.'"

– George Harrison

However, the group began to casually use cannabis and were said to have bought back the drug on occasions to Liverpool. Later, it became well known that Bob Dylan properly introduced the group to cannabis in 1964. The story was recorded in The Love you Make, by Peter Brown, "…Dylan suggested they have a smoke. Brian and The Beatles looked at each other apprehensively. 'We've never smoked marijuana before,' Brian finally admitted. Dylan looked disbelievingly from face to face. 'But what about your song?' he asked. 'The one about getting high?'

"The Beatles were stupefied. 'Which song?' John managed to ask. Dylan said, 'You know...' and then he sang, 'and when I touch you I get high, I get high...'

"John flushed with embarrassment. 'Those aren't the words,' he admitted. 'The words are, 'I can't hide, I can't hide, I can't hide...'"

*The Beatles pose for a strange group portrait,
holding striped umbrellas in Scotland, 1964*

Several accounts recalled Starr was not familiar with the social etiquette of passing the joint around the room and finished it himself. Epstein apparently said, "I'm so high I'm on the ceiling. I'm up on the ceiling."

Paul McCartney told Mal Evans to record his thoughts: "I remember asking Mal, our road manager, for what seemed like years and years, 'Have you got a pencil?' But of course everyone was so stoned they couldn't produce a pencil, let alone a combination of pencil and paper.

"I'd been going through this thing of levels, during the evening. And at each level I'd meet all these people again. 'Hahaha! It's you!' And then I'd metamorphose on to another level. Anyway, Mal gave me this little slip of paper in the morning, and written on it was, 'There are seven levels!' Actually it wasn't bad. Not bad for an amateur. And we pissed ourselves laughing. I mean, 'What the f***'s that? What the f*** are the seven levels?' But looking back, it's actually a pretty succinct comment; it ties in with a lot of major religions but I didn't know that then."

Evans kept the notebooks, which were confiscated by Los Angeles police on his death in 1976 and eventually were lost.

A tired Ringo playing drums in 1965

Paul McCartney relaxing at manager, Brian Epstein's house, 1967

The group had by this point become regular users of cannabis, which by their accounts, made their songwriting and music more philosophical and thoughtful. In 1961, The Beatles were said to have tried cocaine, at a gig they were backing for a rock singer Davy Jones at the Cavern in Liverpool.

Bob Wooler, the Cavern's DJ, recalled, "We didn't have a strong drug scene by any means. Originally, it was just purple hearts, amphetamines, speed or whatever you want to call it. When The Beatles went down south, they sometimes brought back cannabis and gradually the drug scene developed in Liverpool. There was a rare instance of cocaine when Davy Jones, a black rock 'n' roll singer who'd been with The Beatles in Hamburg, appeared at the Cavern. He was a Little Richard/ Derry Wilkie type, very outgoing and bouncy. His big record was an oldie, Amapola, and its lyric about the 'pretty little poppy' must have appealed to him."

McCartney regularly used cocaine. Around the time Sgt. Pepper's Lonely Hearts Club Band was recorded.

"I did cocaine for about a year around the time of Sgt. Pepper. Coke and maybe some grass to balance it out. I was never completely crazy with cocaine. I'd been introduced to it and at first it seemed OK, like anything that's new and stimulating. When you start working your way through it, you start thinking: 'Mmm, this is not so cool an idea,' especially when you start getting those terrible comedowns."

– Paul McCartney in an interview with Uncut magazine, 2004

And when he talked to Barry Miles in McCartney's official autobiography, Many Years From Now, he said,

"At the time cocaine wasn't widely used or easily available, although it had been fashionable in certain sections of society since the 1920s. During the making of Sgt. Pepper Robert Fraser offered them cocaine, heroin, and speedballs – a mixture of the two. Cocaine was the only one of the three that was accepted.

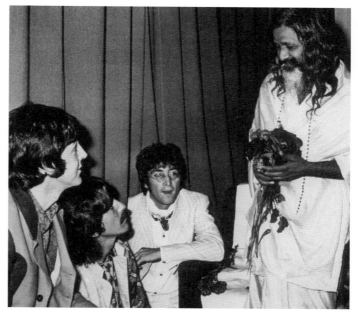

Left to right; Paul McCartney, George Harrison, and John Lennon backstage with the Maharishi Mahesh Yogi after he gave a lecture on transcendental meditation

John Lennon wearing a frilly shirt and a sporran, 1967

"He walked in with a little phial of white powder. 'What's that?' 'Cocaine.' 'S***, that smells just like what the dentist used to give us.' To this day, I swear as kids in Liverpool we were given cocaine to deaden the gums. People say no, that will have been Novocaine, but I think that was much later. I recognize the smell from the dentist; it's a medical smell coke can have. Anyway, that was my first thought about it.

"I liked the paraphernalia. I liked the ritualistic end of it. I was particularly amused by rolling up a pound note. There was a lot of symbolism in that: sniffing it through money! For Sgt. Pepper I used to have a bit of coke and then smoke some grass to balance it out.

"So Robert introduced me to it, and I know the other guys were a bit shocked at me and said, 'Hey, man, you know this is like, "now you're getting into drugs". This is more than pot.' I remember feeling a little bit superior and patting them on the head, symbolically, and saying, 'No. Don't worry, guys. I can handle it.' And as it happened, I could. What I enjoyed was the ritual of meeting someone and them saying, 'Have you seen the toilets in this place?' And you'd know what they meant. 'Oh no, are they particularly good?' And you'd wander out to the toilets and you'd snort a bit of stuff. Robert and I did that for a bit. It wasn't ever too crazy; eventually I just started to think - I think rightly now - that this doesn't work. You've got to put too much in to get too little high out of it. I did it for about a year and I got off it.

"I'd been in a club in London and somebody there had some and I'd snorted it. I remember going to the toilet and I met Jimi Hendrix on the way. 'Jimi! Great, man,' because I love that guy. But then as I hit the toilet, it all wore off! And I started getting this dreadful melancholy. I remember walking back and asking, 'Have you got any more?' because the whole mood had just dropped, the bottom had dropped out, and I remember thinking then it was time to stop it.

George Harrison burns the candle at both ends in 1967

"I thought, this is not clever, for two reasons. Number one, you didn't stay high. The plunge after it was this melancholy plunge, which I was not used to. I had quite a reasonable childhood so melancholy was not really much part of it, even though my mum dying was a very bad period, so for anything that put me in that kind of mood it was like, 'Huh, I'm not paying for this! Who needs that?' The other reason was just a physical thing with the scraunching round the back of the neck, when it would get down the back of your nose, and it would all go dead! This was what reminded me of the dentist. It was exactly the same feeling as the stuff to numb your teeth.

"I remember when I stopped doing it. I went to America just after Pepper came out, and I was thinking of stopping it. And everyone there was taking it, all these music business people, and I thought, no."

In 1965, Lennon and his then wife Cynthia, as well as Harrison and Boyd were invited to dinner by the band's dentist. He famously served them coffee laced with LSD, without his guests' knowledge. It was recalled by Lennon to Jann Wenner, "He laid it on George, me and our wives without telling us at a dinner party at his house. He was a friend of George's, and our dentist at the time. He just put it in our coffee or something. He didn't know what it was, it was just, 'It's all the thing,' with the middle-class London swingers. They had all heard about it and didn't know it was different from pot or pills. And they gave it to us, and he was saying, 'I advise you not to leave,' and we thought he was trying to keep us for an orgy in his house and we didn't want to know."

John and Cynthia Lennon at Heathrow in 1964

The Beatles pose for a photographer in 1965

Signing autographs
for fans

George Harrison of the Beatles with his girlfriend Patti Boyd and Lionel Bart at a party held at the Pickwick Club, 1967

Harrison recalled in The Beatles Anthology, "One night John, Cynthia, Pattie, and I were having dinner at the dentist's house. Later that night we were going to a London nightclub called the Pickwick Club. It was a little restaurant with a small stage where some friends of ours were playing. Klaus Voormann, Gibson Kemp (who became Rory Storm's drummer after we stole Ringo) and a guy called Paddy. They had a little trio.

"After dinner I said to John, 'Let's go - they're going to be on soon,' and John said 'OK,' but the dentist was saying, 'Don't go; you should stay here.' And then he said, 'Well, at least finish your coffee first.' So we finished our coffee and after a while I said again, 'Come on, it's getting late - we'd better go.' The dentist said something to John and John turned to me and said, 'We've had LSD.'

"I just thought, 'Well, what's that? So what? Let's go!'

"This fella was still asking us to stay and it all became a bit seedy - it felt as if he was trying to get something happening in his house; that there was some reason he didn't want us to go. In fact, he had obtained some lysergic acid diethylamide 25. It was, at the time, an unrestricted medication - I seem to recall that I'd heard vaguely about it, but I didn't really know what it was, and we didn't know we were taking it. The bloke had put it in our coffee: mine, John's, Cynthia's, and Pattie's. He didn't take it. He had never had it himself. I'm sure he thought it was an aphrodisiac. I remember his girlfriend had enormous breasts and I think he thought that there was going to be a big gang-bang and that he was going to get to shag everybody. I really think that was his motive.

The Beatles pose together under a large banner that reads 'Help!'

"So the dentist said, 'OK, leave your car here. I'll drive you and then you can come back later.' I said, 'No, no. We'll drive.' And we all got in my car and he came as well, in his car. We got to the nightclub, parked and went in.

"We'd just sat down and ordered our drinks when suddenly I feel the most incredible feeling come over me. It was something like a very concentrated version of the best feeling I'd ever had in my whole life.

"It was fantastic. I felt in love, not with anything or anybody in particular, but with everything. Everything was perfect, in a perfect light, and I had an overwhelming desire to go round the club telling everybody how much I loved them - people I'd never seen before.

"One thing led to another, then suddenly it felt as if a bomb had made a direct hit on the nightclub and the roof had been blown off: 'What's going on here?' I pulled my senses together and I realized that the club had actually closed - all the people had gone, they'd put the lights on, and the waiters were going round bashing the tables and putting the chairs on top of them. We thought, 'Oops, we'd better get out of here!'"

Paul McCartney; with The Beatles, performing live onstage at Ernst Merck Halle on their final German Tour.

Clockwise from top; John Lennon, Ringo Starr, Paul McCartney, and George Harrison pose for a portrait in front of an American Flag in New York City, 1964

In the same title, McCartney recalled the media fuss that followed, "I remember a couple of men from ITN showed up, and then the newscaster arrived: 'Is it true you've had drugs?' They were at my door – I couldn't tell them to go away – so I thought, 'Well, I'm either going to try to bluff this, or I'm going to tell him the truth.' I made a lightning decision: 'Sod it. I'll give them the truth.'

"I spoke to the reporter beforehand, and said, 'You know what's going to happen here: I'm going to get the blame for telling everyone I take drugs. But you're the people who are going to distribute the news.' I said, 'I'll tell you. But if you've got any worries about the news having an effect on kids, then don't show it. I'll tell you the truth, but if you disseminate the whole thing to the public then it won't be my responsibility. I'm not sure I want to preach this but, seeing as you're asking – yeah, I've taken LSD.' I'd had it about four times at the stage, and I told him so. I felt it was reasonable, but it became a big news item."

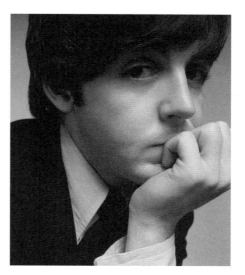

A contemplative photo of McCartney from 1965

The Beatles giving a press conference after receiving their MBEs, Lennon would later give his back

McCartney and Lennon at a press conference in 1965

It was also in 1965 that the band was first exposed to heroin. The director of Help!, Richard Lester, recalled watching two women attempting to coax McCartney into taking the drug. McCartney refused on that occasion, but recalled much later in an interview with Uncut that he had tried it, "I tried heroin just the once. Even then, I didn't realize I'd taken it. I was just handed something, smoked it, then found out what it was. It didn't do anything for me, which was lucky because I wouldn't have fancied heading down that road."

However, this was to differ from his account in his authorised autobiography, Many Years From Now, "I was very frightened of drugs, having a nurse mother, so I was always cautious, thank God as it turned out, because I would be in rooms with guys who would say, 'Do you want to sniff a little heroin?' and I would say, 'Well, just a little.' I did some with Robert Fraser, and some of the boys in the Stones who were doing things like that. I always refer to it as walking through a minefield, and I was lucky because had anyone hit me with a real dose that I loved, I would have been a heroin addict.

"Robert Fraser once said to me, 'Heroin is not addictive. There's no problem with heroin addiction, even if it is addictive, you've just got to have a lot of money. The problem with heroin is when you can't pay for it.' Which of course is absolute bullshit! You're a junkie, of course you are. This was the way he put it to me and for a second I was almost taken in but then my northern savvy kicked in and said, 'Now don't go for all of this. This is all very exotic and romantic but don't go for all of it.' There was always a little corner, at the back of my brain, that 'knock! knock! knock!' on the door – 'Stop!'

Ringo Starr performs on the set of the movie 'Help!'

Lennon wearing his trademark glasses in 1967

"A lot of his friends messed around with heroin. A lot of his lords and ladies were heroin addicts and had been for many many years. And give Robert his due, he knew I wasn't that keen. He knew I wasn't a nutter for that kind of stuff. So I did sniff heroin with him once, but I said afterwards, 'I'm not sure about this, man. It didn't really do anything for me,' and he said, 'In that case, I won't offer you again.' And I didn't take it again. I was often around it when they'd all be doing it. They'd repair to the toilet and I'd say, 'I'm all right, thanks, no.' One of the most difficult things about that period was the peer pressure to do that."

It was reported Lennon was hooked on heroin between 1968-1969, and McCartney said,

"He was getting into harder drugs than we'd been into and so his songs were taking on more references to heroin. Until that point we had made rather mild, oblique references to pot or LSD. But now John started talking about fixes and monkeys and it was harder terminology which the rest of us weren't into. We were disappointed that he was getting into heroin because we didn't really know how we could help him. We just hoped it wouldn't go too far. In actual fact, he did end up clean but this was the period when he was on it. It was a tough period for John, but often that adversity and craziness can lead to good art, as I think it did in this case."

The Beatles, performing live onstage with
The Dirty Mac on the set of Rock 'n' Roll
Circus, 1968

Lennon himself admitted he was addicted for a couple of years, "Heroin. It just was not too much fun. I never injected it or anything. We sniffed a little when we were in real pain. I mean we just couldn't - people were giving us such a hard time. And I've had so much shit thrown at me and especially at Yoko. People like Peter Brown in our office, he comes down and shakes my hand and doesn't even say hello to her. Now that's going on all the time. And we get in so much pain that we have to do something about it. And that's what happened to us. We took H because of what The Beatles and their pals were doing to us. And we got out of it. They didn't set down to do it, but things came out of that period. And I don't forget."

In 1967, Epstein and The Beatles added their names to the Times newspaper advertisement calling for the legalization of cannabis. The following year, Lennon and Ono, who was pregnant, were arrested for possession while staying with Starr in London. Lennon pleaded guilty.

That same year, The Beatles publicly promoted meditation in place of drugs, with a statement on August 26th after the end of the Summer of Love. Lennon had stopped taking LSD but said, "A little mushroom or peyote is not beyond my scope, you know, maybe twice a year or something. But acid is a chemical. People are taking it, though, even though you don't hear about it anymore. But people are still visiting the cosmos. It's just that nobody talks about it; you get sent to prison...

John Lennon took a cocktail of illegal drugs during the 1960s and 1970s

John Lennon's behavior became more and more bizarre, perhaps linked to his heroin and LSD use

John Lennon sings in bed during his Protest for Peace

"I've never met anybody who's had a flashback. I've never had a flashback in my life and I took millions of trips in the Sixties, and I've never met anybody who had any problem. I've had bad trips and other people have had bad trips, but I've had a bad trip in real life. I've had a bad trip on a joint. I can get paranoid just sitting in a restaurant. I don't have to take anything.

"Acid is only real life in Cinemascope. Whatever experience you had is what you would have had anyway. I'm not promoting, all you committees out there, and I don't use it because it's chemical, but all the garbage about what it did to people is garbage."

– *John Lennon, 1980, as printed in* All We Are Saying

"The Beatles had gone beyond comprehension. We were smoking marijuana for breakfast. We were well into marijuana and nobody could communicate with us, because we were just glazed eyes, giggling all the time."

– *John Lennon*

Ono suffered a miscarriage in 1969, which was reported by some to be because of heroin. Many years later, on the BBC Radio 4 Programme Desert Island Discs, Ono claimed "Luckily we never injected because both of us were totally scared about needles. So that probably saved us. And the other thing that saved us was our connection was not very good."

In 1969, Harrison and his wife were also arrested for possession of cannabis. They claimed London's drugs squad had planted the drugs.

George Harrison leaving court after being fined £250
for possession of cannabis, 1969

Born Brian Samuel Epstein, The Beatles manager rode the wave of drugs, fame, and euphoria with his band. Indeed, their early success had been credited to Epstein and McCartney said, "If anyone was the Fifth Beatle, it was Brian."

Epstein kept his homosexuality a secret throughout his public life, although The Beatles knew. Homosexuality was a criminal offence in England and Wales, and right up to the year he died. Being Jewish probably did not make it any easier. His sexual orientation was not known until years after his death.

On seeing the band perform Epstein said, "They were rather scruffily dressed, in the nicest possible way, or I should say in the most attractive way: black leather jackets, jeans, long hair of course."

When Epstein started managing the band, McCartney said they knew that he was gay but did not care. It was reported that Lennon made sarcastic remarks about Epstein's orientation to Epstein and to his friends, but then defended him against any ridicule or comments from outside the group.

In Best's autobiography, he recalled Epstein expressed "very fond admiration" for Best and apparently said, "Would you find it embarrassing if I ask you to stay in a hotel overnight?" Best said he was not interested and the topic was dropped.

Rumors also abound regarding Lennon's relationship with Epstein, although he rebuked them in an interview with Playboy magazine in 1980, "Well, it was almost a love affair, but not quite. It was never consummated... but we did have a pretty intense relationship."

Brian Epstein, circa 1967

John Lennon plays the guitar in a hotel room in Paris, while Brian Epstein examines a photographic contact sheet, January 16th, 1964

During the sixties, Epstein became dependent on sleeping pills and amphetamine. Like Lennon, McCartney, Harrison, and Starr, he had begun taking Preludin to stay awake during the concert tours. It was reported that by the mid-60s Epstein was addicted, with McCartney recalling Epstein would grind his jaws, and once said, "Ugghhh, the pills" to McCartney.

On one holiday, Epstein attempted to clean up by attending the Priory Clinic.

In the days before his death, Epstein's assistant Peter Brown spoke to him over the phone saying that he sounded "very groggy," and suggested that he take a train in place of driving to his next engagement.

Brown never heard from him again.

Epstein was found in his bedroom by his butler, in his pajamas surrounded by paperwork. He had taken Carbitral, a form of barbiturate or sleeping pill in order to sleep, but in combination with alcohol it was lethal. To allow Epstein's family privacy, The Beatles did not attend his funeral. They attended a memorial service a few weeks later.

Harrison once said that the MBE stood for 'Mister Brian Epstein.'

John Lennon and his wife Cynthia arriving at the memorial service of Brian Epstein.

Paul McCartney and his girlfriend Jane Asher just after hearing of the death of Brian Epstein

Brian Epstein in a TV studio, circa 1965

The Beatles manager
Brian Epstein in a
Granada Television studio
in Manchester during a
recording of Late Scene
Extra, November 25th,
1963

A general view of the White Album room is seen at the Beatlemania exhibition on May 28th, 2009 in Hamburg, Germany

Let It Be

Following the death of Epstein in 1967 and the band's departure from the Sergeant Pepper era, things became more complicated musically and politically within the group.

After audiences and critics panned Magical Mystery Tour, the group persisted with the release of the album, which helped redeem the group somewhat. The first weeks of its release saw a new record set, for the highest initial sales of any Capitol LP. It is still the only Capitol compilation included in the group's canon of studio albums. Then came the Beatles White Album, named because of its completely blank cover by pop artist Richard Hamilton.

During this time, feeling lost and unsure without Epstein, the band sought solace in Maharishi Mahesh Yogi. By attending another course in India, they initially found some solace that led to the group composing a number of songs. But this retreat also led to the group's disappointment in the Yogi's authenticity after some months, with McCartney claiming, "We made a mistake. We thought there was more to him than there was."

Tensions mounted while recording the album, which were exacerbated by Lennon's insistence on Ono's attendance at the sessions. The group had a long-established rule that wives and girlfriends were not to accompany the artists to the studio.

Of the White Album, which was recorded in October 1968, Lennon said, "Every track is an individual track; there isn't any Beatles music on it. [It's] John and the band, Paul and the band, George and the band." McCartney recalled that the album "wasn't a pleasant one to make."

Despite the tension, the album drew more than two million advance orders, and sold nearly four million copies in the US in little over a month. Its commercial success, however, was not matched by critical acclaim, which was mostly mixed, but none of it highly positive. Over time, however, critical opinion became more positive and in 2003 Rolling Stone ranked it as the tenth greatest album of all time.

The Maharishi had considerable influence over The Beatles with his transcendental teachings

*A view of graffiti tributes written by members of the public
at the entrance to the Abbey Road recording studios*

Everybodies talking bout
Bagism   Ministers   resolution   John + Yoko
Shagism   sinisters   evolution   Timmy Leary
Dragism   bannisters   masturbation   Tommy Smothers
Madism   cannisters   flagellation   Bobby Dylan
Lagism   Bishop +   regulation   Tommy Cooper
tagism   Fishops   integration   Derek Taylor
This-ism   Rabbicer   meditations   Norma Mailen
That-ism   Popeyes   United Nations Alan Ginsberg
              Bye Byes.   Congratulation Hare Krishna
                                            Hare Krana

All we are saying is give peace a chance.

John Lennon's original lyrics for 'Give Peace a Chance'

The Yellow Submarine album followed in January 1969, but by this point, sadly for fans, it was the beginning of the end for The Beatles.

Let It Be is the 12th and final studio record issued by The Beatles and was issued shortly after the group announced their break up in 1970.

The majority of the album had been laid down in the studio in January of 1969, which was before Abbey Road was recorded and released. As such, debate still rages over which is actually The Beatles final album. Regardless, when Let it Be was released, it served as the much-loved album accompanied by the film of the same title in 1970.

Because of the tension between the band members, it was a surprise to Martin that McCartney had asked him to produce another album, Abbey Road, which was recorded in July of 1969.

On America's Independence Day, the 4th of July, Lennon released the first solo single from a Beatle titled Give Peace a Chance.

And in August 1969, the group was together in the studio for the last time. On the 20th of September, Lennon announced to the group he was leaving the band and agreed not to make it public until the album Abbey Road was released.

On the 26th of September, Abbey Road topped the charts, staying at Number one in the UK for 17 weeks. It went on to sell four million copies within three months.

THE BEATLES

Let it Be was originally intended to be a one-hour television show called Beatles at Work, which would be filmed and recorded at Twickenham Film Studios. Director Lindsay-Hogg was due to film in January of 1969, but Martin recalled it was "not at all a happy recording experience. It was a time when relations between The Beatles were at their lowest."

Lennon later said the sessions were "hell ... the most miserable ... on Earth," and Harrison claimed them, "the low of all-time."

Of the album, Lennon told Rolling Stone magazine, "We couldn't get into it. It was just a dreadful, dreadful feeling at Twickenham Studios. You couldn't make music at eight in the morning, in a strange place with people filming you, and colored lights ... I was stoned all the time and I just didn't give a s***."

The film Let it Be is well known for its portrayal of the band breaking up, with conflicts between members of the band. With the difficult atmosphere, the sessions grew increasingly challenging. The group displayed a lack of attention and enthusiasm, with McCartney attempting to rally his bandmates. His behavior was viewed as controlling and, in a famous scene in the film, Harrison had a heated argument with McCartney.

"We started Let It Be in January 1969 at Twickenham Studios, under the working title Get Back. Michael Lindsay-Hogg was the director. The idea was that you'd see The Beatles rehearsing, jamming, getting their act together, and then finally performing somewhere in a big end-of-show concert. We would show how the whole process worked. I remember I had an idea for the final scene, which would be a massive tracking shot, forever and ever, and then we'd be in the concert.

"The original idea was to go on an ocean liner and get away from the world; you would see us rehearsing and then you'd finally see the pay-off. But we ended up in Twickenham. I think it was a safer situation for the director and everybody. Nobody was that keen on going on an ocean liner anyway. It was getting a bit fraught between us at that point, because we'd been together a long time and cracks were beginning to appear."

– Paul McCartney, The Beatles Anthology

George Harrison on set of the film A Hard Day's Night

Apparently, there was an even more heated argument between Harrison and Lennon, which is not shown in the film. Harrison, tired of Lennon's lack of enthusiasm and creative difficulties, rowed with him. According to some reports, they exchanged punches, although Harrison said in an interview with the Daily Express Newspaper, "There was no punch-up. We just fell out." After Harrison left that day, the remaining members attempted to continue the session.

"For me, to come back into the winter of discontent with The Beatles in Twickenham was very unhealthy and unhappy. But I can remember feeling quite optimistic about it. I thought, 'OK, it's the New Year and we have a new approach to recording.' I think the first couple of days were OK, but it was soon quite apparent that it was just the same as it had been when we were last in the studio, and it was going to be painful again. There was a lot of trivia and games being played.

"As everybody knows, we never had much privacy – and now they were filming us rehearsing. One day there was a row going on between Paul and me. It's actually in the film: you can see where he's saying, 'Well, don't play this,' and I'm saying, 'I'll play whatever you want me to play, or I won't play at all if you don't want me to play. Whatever it is that will please you, I'll do it...'

"They were filming us having a row. It never came to blows, but I thought, 'What's the point of this? I'm quite capable of being relatively happy on my own and I'm not able to be happy in this situation. I'm getting out of here.'

"Everybody had gone through that. Ringo had left at one point. I know John wanted out. It was a very, very difficult, stressful time, and being filmed having a row as well was terrible. I got up and I thought, 'I'm not doing this any more. I'm out of here.'"

– *George Harrison, The Beatles Anthology*

George Harrison and his wife Pattie Boyd on their way to Nice, 1969

George Harrison on stage in 1969

*Left to right; Ringo,
Paul, George, and John
at a press conference
on final German tour*

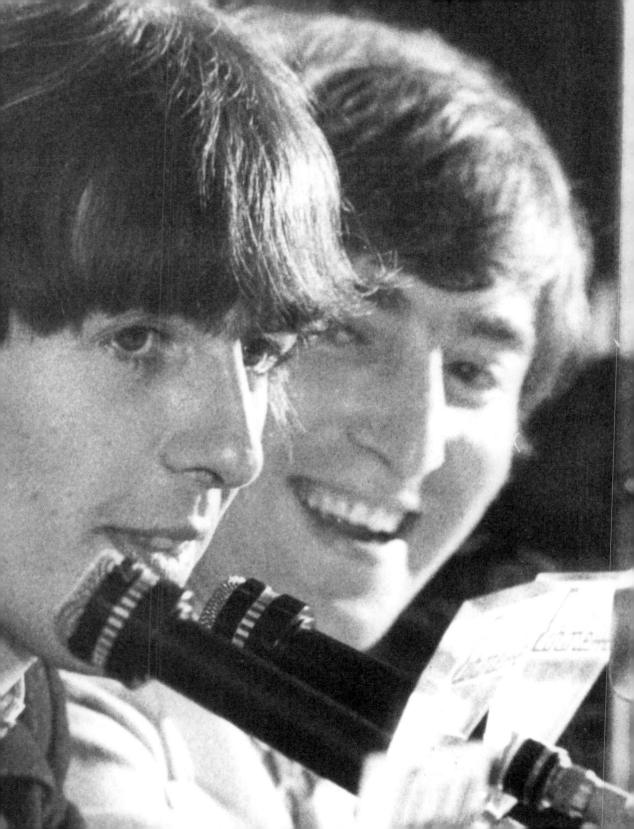

Annoyed by McCartney and Lennon, Harrison walked out for five days. When he returned, he gave the band members an ultimatum, to finish a new album using the songs they'd recorded for the television program and to stop recording at Twickenham and go to Apple Studios for a fresh start. Harrison also invited keyboardist Billy Preston for the sessions, and was the only musician to get an acknowledgement on a Beatles release.

"George left because Paul and he were having a heated discussion. They weren't getting on that day and George decided to leave, but he didn't tell John or me or Paul. There'd been some tension going down in the morning, and arguments would go on anyway, so none of us realized until we went to lunch that George had gone home. When we came back he still wasn't there, so we started jamming violently. Paul was playing his bass into the amp and John was off, and I was playing some weird drumming that I hadn't done before. I don't play like that as a rule. Our reaction was really, really interesting at the time. And Yoko jumped in, of course; she was there."

– *Ringo Starr, The Beatles Anthology*

Further conflict followed with disagreements over who should manage the group's finances, with Lennon, Harrison, and Starr favoring the Rolling Stones' financial advisor, Allen Klein and McCartney favoring John Eastmen, the brother of Linda, his now wife. Both were temporarily appointed but after more conflict, Klein was give sole management of the band.

Meanwhile, the album that was originally titled Get Back, renamed Let it Be, was still to be finished, with another single recorded in January of 1970. Lennon did not join.

George Harrison taking some time out in Denmark in 1969

John Lennon performing with the newly-formed Plastic Ono Band at the Lyceum Theatre, London, 1969

On April 10th, 1970, McCartney announced his departure from the band, and a week later released his own self-titled solo album.

Eventually, on the May 8th, Let It Be was released. The final album was not completely to McCartney's satisfaction. The documentary film of the same name also followed that month; with Sunday Telegraph critic Penelope Gilliatt writing that it was "a very bad film and a touching one ... about the breaking apart of this reassuring, geometrically perfect, once apparently ageless family of siblings."

Unfortunately, the disbanding of The Beatles continued to be messy, with McCartney filing a lawsuit for the dissolution of The Beatles' contractual partnership on December 31st, 1970. Legal disputes continued long after the band dissolved, resulting in it not being formally dissolved until four years later.

Much later, in 2003, McCartney announced plans to re-release a newly produced version of the album, closer to what he had originally intended for the project. Let It Be... Naked was released in November 2003, in a two-disc format featuring re-mixed songs without the spoken passages and orchestral dubs from the original. This version received mixed reviews also; with some fond of the simpler re-mixes and others considering it a shame the humorous spoken word was removed.

An Evening News night special headline announces Paul McCartney's statement on the Beatles split

Paul McCartney with his wife Linda near London's Law Courts, where he legally tried to 'break up' the band, 1971

John Lennon and his wife Yoko Ono answer the door to their fans during the time a court had given Paul McCartney the go ahead to further his intention to break up the band

A sad time for Beatles fans worldwide, Let it Be was
bittersweet for many. It was a great album to close the
band's career, but it was also marred in disagreements
and relationship woes. The relationships between the
band members grew in time, though, and the title
and lyrics of the album sums up the fans and
The Beatles' feelings on the period: Let it Be.

Paul McCartney with his new band, Wings, in 1970

Linda McCartney,
Paul McCartney, and
Denny Laine of Wings
recording in London,
England in
November 1973

Lennon's Murder

O n the 8th of December 1980, John Lennon was murdered. The morning began in fairly usual style for Lennon. With his wife, Yoko Ono, Lennon left their home at the Dakota Building on the Upper West Side of Manhattan, New York City. The couple ate breakfast at Café La Fortuna, where Lennon ordered eggs benedict.

Annie Leibovitz autographs her iconic Rolling Stone cover photo featuring John Lennon and Yoko Ono

On arrival back at their apartment, they greeted photographer Annie Liebovitz, who famously took photographs of a clothed Ono and a naked Lennon, curled up like a baby around his wife. The shoot was for Rolling Stone magazine, and would later grace the cover six weeks after his passing. Leibovitz had promised Lennon that a photo with Ono would make the cover of the magazine, even though she said, "Nobody wanted [Ono] on the cover" and she had tried to capture photographs of him on his own.

A short while later Dave Sholin, a journalist and DJ with a San Francisco network, RKO Radio, arrived to interview Lennon. He said that when the interview ended Lennon told him, "I consider that my work won't be finished until I'm dead and buried and I hope that's a long, long time."

When Lennon left the apartment, around 5pm, he and Ono were looking for the car that was there to take them to the Record Plant recording studio. Lennon talked with one fan, outside waiting, Paul Goresh. Goresh said of that moment with Lennon, "As he was talking to me the guy with the overcoat approached him from the left.

"He didn't say a word, he just held the album [Lennon's Double Fantasy] out in front of John who turned to him and said, 'Do you want it signed?' And the guy nodded. He didn't say a word.

"I snapped a couple of pictures. He nodded and he took the album and just backed away."

Lennon often stopped to meet fans and sign autographs outside the Dakota Building.

John Lennon and Yoko Ono shortly before Lennon was shot and killed in New York, NY in December, 1980

The couple asked Sholin for a lift to the studio as there was no car to be seen. As they drove and talked, Sholin said Lennon talked of McCartney, "He says, 'Well he's like a brother. I love him. Families... we certainly have our ups and downs and our quarrels. But at the end of the day when it's all said and done I would do anything for him, I think he would do anything for me.'"

At the studio, Lennon and Ono worked on her song Walking on Thin Ice. Afterwards, they were driven by limousine to 72nd street. Ono reported asking Lennon, "I said, 'Shall we go to a restaurant before we go home?' He said, 'No I want to see Sean [their five-year-old son] before he goes to sleep.' I said, 'He's probably asleep by now.'"

"And the car stopped, we got out and it was... really terrible."

As the limousine pulled up outside the Dakota Building, at approximately 10:50 pm, Ono stepped out followed by Lennon. Three shots hit Lennon in the back, which caused him to spin around. Another shot hit him on the shoulder and a fifth shot missed him.

Lennon staggered up the steps of the building and said, "I'm shot," before he collapsed.

Policemen Steve Spiro and Peter Cullen, who were at 72nd Street and Broadway when they heard a report of shots fired, were the first on the scene. The second team arrived a few minutes later and rushed Lennon to the Roosevelt Hospital's emergency room. He was pronounced dead on arrival at 11:07 pm. Some conflicting reports state the time of death as 11:15 pm. Lennon died of hypovolemic shock, caused by loss of blood. It was reported by several hospital staff and Lynn that The Beatles song All My Loving came on over the hospital's sound system at the time he was pronounced dead.

Because of the bullets used, which expand on entry and displace the tissue around the wound, the surgeons reported that even if Lennon was shot in the hospital they would have been unable to save him.

Front page of Tuesday, December 9th, 1980, edition of the Daily News

Fans of John Lennon holding a vigil after he was shot dead

At the emergency room, Doctor Stephan Lynn said, "Through the doors two police officers came in carrying a body over their shoulders. It was lifeless.

"We positioned the body on a stretcher in front of us. It was clear that there were three gunshot wounds in the left upper chest and one to the left arm.

"As part of our normal routine we took his identification out of his clothing and it said John Lennon but the nurses said, 'This doesn't look like John Lennon, it can't be.'

"What we found was that all of the blood vessels that left the heart, the aorta and all of its branches had been destroyed.

"We tried to find a place where we could stop the bleeding.

"I literally held John Lennon's heart in my hand and massaged it to try to get it going again. We transfused blood but it was clear that with all off the vessels destroyed there would be nothing we could do."

Lennon was pronounced dead after losing over 80 percent of his blood. Lynn recalled, "I think everyone of us in the room suddenly realized what we were dealing with. A lot of people began to cry.

"We reminded the staff not to say anything to anybody until an appropriate press announcement had been made. We told the staff they couldn't sell their uniforms that might be bloodstained."

Then Lynn had the difficult job of informing Ono. He said, "Her first response was, 'It's not true, you're lying, it can't be, I don't believe you.' She was laying on the floor, she was hitting her head against the floor. She was incredibly emotional. It was when a nurse brought in John Lennon's wedding ring and gave it to her that she accepted her husband was dead.

"And I was touched by the first thing she said, 'My son Sean is still awake. He's probably sitting in front of the TV set. Please delay making the announcement so I can get home and make certain I tell him what happened before he sees it on TV.'"

The next day Ono issued a statement, "There is no funeral for John. John loved and prayed for the human race. Please pray the same for him."

A mourner places a bouquet among other items including an oil painting arrayed outside the Dakota apartments on 72nd St. and Central Park West, Lennon's, home

Yoko Ono leaving the hospital after her husband John Lennon had been shot dead

Following the tragic news of Lennon's death, there were police statements and eyewitness accounts of the shooting.

The officers reported what they'd witnessed before taking Lennon to the hospital. Spiro recalled, "There was a man pointing into the vestibule and he said, 'That's the man doing the shooting.' I peeked in and saw a man with his hands up. So I threw this guy up against the wall and at that point Jose [Perdomo, the Dakota Building's doorman] says to me, 'He shot John Lennon.'"

The man who shot John Lennon was Mark Chapman, a 25-year-old security guard from Honolulu, Hawaii. He had previously journeyed to New York to murder Lennon, three months earlier, but returned home after changing his mind.

This time, Chapman had intent and did not change his mind. He waited outside the Dakota Building from mid-morning and, according to Chapman, had approached Lennon's five-year-old son Sean and nanny Helen Seaman, managing to touch the child's hand.

The police officers who arrived and Sholin, the journalist who had driven Lennon earlier, witnessed Chapman reading the paperback book the Catcher in the Rye by J.D. Salinger.

The Dakota Building's doorman was ex-CIA agent Jose Sanjenis Perdomo. Perdomo and a cab driver who witnessed the shooting said they saw Chapman waiting for Lennon. Perdomo said he shouted at Chapman, "Do you know what you've done?" He said Chapman calmly replied, "Yes, I just shot John Lennon."

Daily News front page dated December 10th, 1980

*Mark David Chapman was arrested for
Lennon's murder in December 1980*

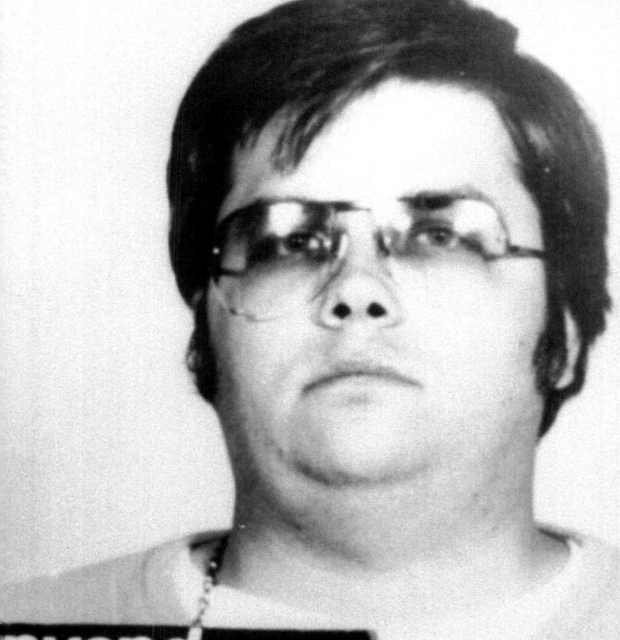

Crowds gathered outside
the home of John Lennon
in New York after the news
that he had been shot
dead

The Charter Arms .38 Special used by Mark David Chapman to kill John Lennon

Chapman was later said to have fired five hollow-point bullets at him from a Charter Arms .38 Special revolver in rapid succession at close range.

Various statements came in from the New York Police Department and across media that Chapman had called out "Mr. Lennon" and dropped into a 'combat stance.'

Chapman has said he does not remember calling out Lennon's name before he fired, but in an interview in 1992 with American television talk show host, Barbara Walters, he admitted he took a combat stance.

He said the reason for shooting Lennon was because of the rock star's comment about The Beatles being 'more popular than Jesus' and labeled it blasphemy. He also said he disagreed with Lennon's songs God and Imagine, in particular because of Lennon's wealth and his lyric 'Imagine no possessions.' By the time he stood before the judge in court, six psychiatrists had determined him psychotic and three declared him delusional. Chapman had said the book was his statement, and on hearing his sentence, he rose and read a passage from the Catcher in the Rye:

"Anyway, I keep picturing all these little kids playing some game in this big field of rye and all. Thousands of little kids, and nobody's around – nobody big, I mean – except me. And I'm standing on the edge of some crazy cliff. What I have to do, I have to catch everybody if they start to go over the cliff – I mean if they're running and they don't look where they're going I have to come out from somewhere and catch them. That's all I do all day. I'd just be the catcher in the rye and all."

Chapman pleaded guilty to second-degree murder. He was sentenced to 20 years to life, and is still in prison.

Lennon's body was cremated two days later at Ferncliff Cemetery in Hartsdale, New York. Ono later scattered his ashes in New York's Central Park.

Yoko Ono is helped by David Geffen as she leaves Roosevelt Hospital after learning her husband, John Lennon, had died

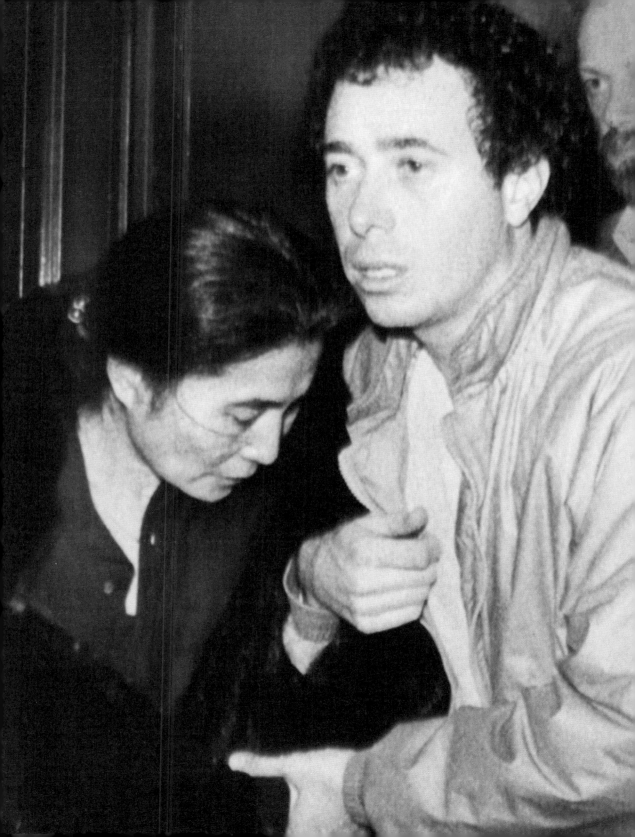

*The hearse carrying the body of John Lennon parked outside the
Frank E. Campbell funeral home, New York City, December 1980*

The Rolling Stone magazine paid tribute to Lennon, in its January 22nd, 1981
issue, with the photographs taken by Leibovitz the day he died. The iconic image
of Lennon and Ono was on the cover, and the publication ran a series of articles,
letters, and photos commemorating his life, music, and death.

Dedications and tributes flowed from his peers, friends, music industry insiders,
and fans. Lennon's death caused an overwhelming outpouring of grief around
the world. In New York, fans gathered at the Dakota building and chanted for
him. Ono asked the crowd to re-convene in Central Park the next Sunday for ten
minutes of silent prayer. The following Sunday, December 14th, 1980, Ono's
request was met by millions of people worldwide, who paused for ten minutes of
silence to remember Lennon.

For the same ten-minute silence, in his hometown Liverpool, 30,000 people
gathered and over 225,000 gathered in Central Park, and radio stations in New
York also went off the air.

"It was a staggering moment when I heard the news. Lennon was a most talented
man and, above all, a gentle soul."

– Frank Sinatra

"I can't take it in. John was a great man who'll be remembered for his unique
contributions to art, music, and world peace."

– Paul McCartney

*The body of John Lennon is taken into Frank E. Campbell
funeral home, Madison Ave. and 81st St. in a body bag*

Fans hold vigil outside of the Dakota Apartments

Fans were despairing, and at least two Beatles fans committed suicide after his murder. Ono made a second appeal, asking mourners to not give in. Ono also released a solo album in 1981, titled Season of Glass, which displayed a photo of Lennon's blood-stained glasses.

Also in 1981, Harrison released a tribute song All Those Years Ago, featuring Starr and McCartney. McCartney then included his tribute, Here Today, to Lennon on his album Tug of War in 1982.

More artists recorded tributes and farewells for Lennon. Elton John, who had recorded the number-one hit Whatever Gets You Thru The Night with Lennon, worked with lyricist, Bernie Taupin to compose Empty Garden (Hey Hey Johnny). The track appeared on his 1982 album, Jump Up!

In August of the same year, when Elton John performed to a sell-out arena in Madison Square Garden, New York, he invited Ono and Sean on stage.

Then-President Jimmy Carter said, "John Lennon helped create the mood and the music of the time."

The Beatles' New York concert promoter, Sid Bernstein, said Lennon was "the Bach, Beethoven, the Rachmaninoff of our time."

Written by Freddie Mercury, Queen performed the song Life Is Real from the album Hot Space (1982), in his memory.

"We have lost a genius of the spirit."

– Norman Mailer

Fans protest at Lennon's vigil

In 1985, the City of New York created a memorial space for Lennon, in an area of Central Park where he had frequently walked. Known as Strawberry Fields, countries from around the world donated trees to the memorial area as a sign of unity. Naples, Italy also donated the mosaic that sits as centerpiece, called Imagine.

In 1991, Lennon was honored with a Grammy Lifetime Achievement Award.

Cities around the world have continued to show tributes to Lennon. Cuba has a bronze statue of Lennon in a Havana park, Japan opened a Lennon Museum in the city of Saitama, Liverpool's airport is now Liverpool John Lennon Airport, Mexico placed a plaque in honor of his contribution to music, culture and peace, and in Iceland a memorial named Imagine Peace Tower was dedicated by Ono. Every year, on the anniversary of his death, the memorial projects a beam of light into the sky in his memory.

In Hollywood, a memorial ceremony is held every 8th of December in front of the Capitol Records building and candles are lit in front of his Walk of Fame Star.

New York City's Rock and Roll Hall of Fame held a John Lennon exhibit in 2009, displaying many personal effects, as well as the clothes he was wearing when he was murdered – still in the brown paper bag from Roosevelt Hospital.

And every 8th of December, Ono still places a lit candle in the window of Lennon's room in the Dakota Building.

"I'm not afraid of death because I don't believe in it.

It's just getting out of one car, and into another"

– *John Lennon*

This corner of the park honors musician
and Beatles member John Lennon who
lived in New York when he was killed

A floral tribute at the feet of a statue of John
Lennon on Mathew Street near the Cavern
Club in Liverpool 21 years after his death

HOMEMADE · PATISSERIE · SANDWICHES

Skiffle Group
John E Paul
Hounds
Squire Richard
Colbecks Jazz Band
LIAM
Terry
Sextet
The Locomotive
Show Band
The
Bitter Suite
Hispanos
Atacama
MAY
Lemon
Wood
The Collemans
Jazz Band
Days
The
King Bees
The Fallons
Mitchell
Station
Jill Martin
Ebony Blush

The
Thunderbirds
The
Hungry 1's
The
Illusions
ry Walker
he Rain
The
Interludes
The
Hi Cats
The
Incident
Hy-Katz
Skiffle Group
In B

Futureworld33

Dhyana

Cards, candles, and pictures placed there by hundreds of fans adorn a memorial at Strawberry Fields in Central Park on the 30th anniversary of the death of John Lennon

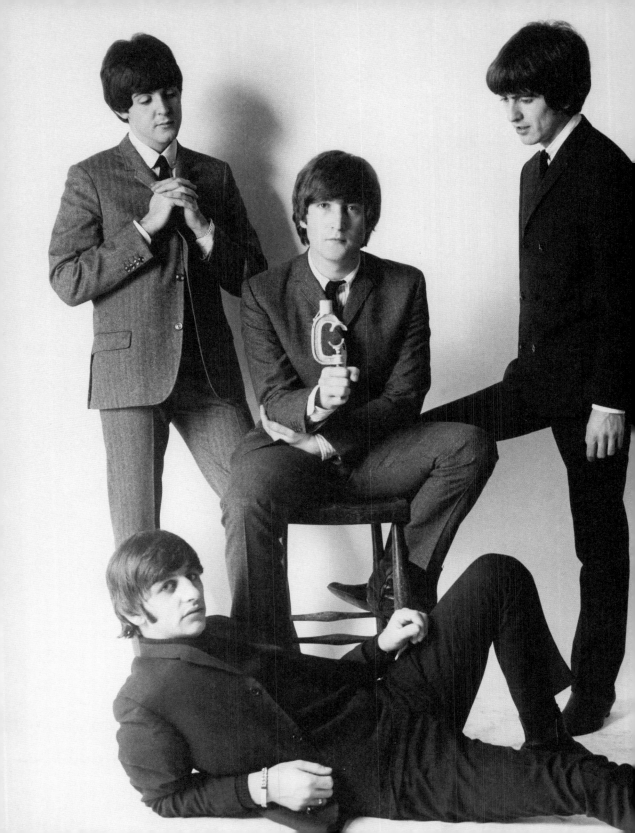

The Beatles: A Legacy

From humble beginnings as schoolboys in Liverpool, The Beatles rose to global fame and recognition as the rock band that captured the hearts and imaginations of the youth of the 60s.

The Beatles challenged the sound of group acts of the time and combined their love of rhythm and blues, Motown, jazz, and country to create a completely different and exciting genre.

Like their hero, Elvis Presley, The Beatles shocked conservative England and America, bringing a new music to the generation growing up. Their innovations and experimental approach to music would continue to surprise, inspire, and influence new generations of musicians for years to come.

Early Beatles pose for photographers in 1963

An early photo shoot with The Beatles in 1962

Backstage Beatles in 1963

As the former associate editor of Rolling Stone magazine said, The Beatles were "artists who broke through the constraints of their time period to come up with something that was unique and original ... [I]n the form of popular music, no one will ever be more revolutionary, more creative and more distinctive." In this way, he likened them to the painter and artist Picasso.

Picking up where Presley left off, The Beatles triggered a huge reaction in the US, leading what would become known as the British Invasion of the US, paving the way for more British acts to break the difficult transatlantic cultural and musical barrier.

Causing riots and hysteria wherever they went, the young musicians made a big impact on their audiences and their fan base.

Paul McCartney during a rehearsal at the Cavern Club, Liverpool, February 1st, 1963

When the group played the Shea Stadium show, in 1965 as part of their US tour, it attracted an estimated 55,600 people, which was then the largest audience in concert history.

It was described a "major breakthrough ... a giant step toward reshaping the concert business" by Beatles biographer Bob Spitz.

And like their cultural change maker hero Elvis, the band re-shaped the look and fashion of the time, not just the music. Young men copied their look, their clothing, and haircuts, making it a sign of youthful rebellion.

But if Beatlemania began as a fashionable trend or fad, the longevity of the group cannot be questioned. Spanning three decades, their music was as relevant in the 80s as it was in the 60s. For, despite the band breaking up in 1970, the re-releases and re-mixes that followed in the 80s, in addition to the solo work of the four members, continued to make an impression, sell records, and speak to the hearts and minds of millions.

The Beatles answer questions regarding their Shea Stadium concert at a press conference on August 23rd, 1965

The Beatles at Shea Stadium, August, 1965

Excited young Beatles fans hoping for a glimpse of their musical heroes during the filming of the musical Help!

For many, they changed they way people listened to music and how they incorporated it into their lives. The Beatles inspired and started the first music videos, which continue to be a must-have for today's artists.

Music became a visual and hearing experience. As Beatlemania grew and matured, the band became icons of bohemian life, of cultural and social revolution. They spoke out on drugs, war and, through their own growth and experience in life, they reassessed their own views on the treatment of women, children, and animals.

They also represented sexual liberation, gay rights, and environmentalism.

It was an exciting time for the music industry. Much cultural change has developed since within the music industry, from artists and performers.

In addition to their inspiring cultural change, they were recognized with an extraordinary number of achievements and awards.

The Beatles on stage at the Coliseum, Washington

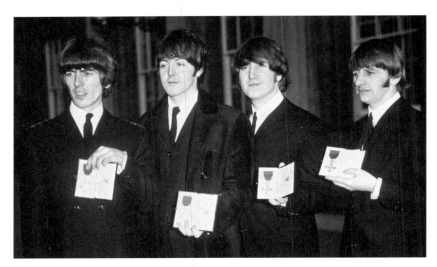

*Left to right; George Harrison, Paul McCartney,
John Lennon, Ringo Starr collecting their MBEs*

In 1965, Queen Elizabeth II appointed Lennon,
McCartney, Harrison, and Starr Members of the
Order of the British Empire (MBE). The Fab
Four also won the 1971 Academy Award for Best
Original Song Score for Let it Be.

They were awarded six diamond albums, 24 multi-
platinum albums, 39 platinum albums, and 45 gold
albums in the US. In the UK, The Beatles have
four multi-platinum albums, four platinum albums,
eight gold albums, and one silver album. They
were also recipients of 15 Ivor Novello Awards,
seven Grammy Awards, and were inducted into the
Rock and Roll Hall of Fame in 1988.

They became the best-selling band ever.

With an estimated one billion units worldwide, the
group have had more number one albums on the
British charts, with 15 recorded. They have also
sold more singles in the UK, with 21.9 million,
than any other act known.

In 2008, they ranked number one in Billboard
magazine's list of the all-time most successful
Hot 100 artists. In 2012, they still held the record
for most number one hits on the Hot 100 chart
with 20 songs.

The Beatles have sold 177 million units in the
US, more than any other artist, as stated by the
Recording Industry Association of America.

*Allen Livingston, President of Capital Records
presents the Beatles with a Gold Record*

THE BEATLES: EXTRAORDINARY FACTS AND FIGURES

The Beatles have had more number one singles than any other musical group (23 in Australia, 23 in The Netherlands, 22 in Canada, 21 in Norway, 20 in the U.S., and 18 in Sweden).

Lennon and McCartney are the most successful songwriters in history, based on song chart positions, with 32 number one singles in the U.S. for McCartney, and 26 for Lennon (23 of which were written together). Lennon was responsible for 29 Number One singles in the UK, and McCartney was responsible for 28 (25 of which were written together).

The next week, April 11th, 1964, The Beatles held fourteen positions on the Billboard Hot 100. Before The Beatles, the highest number of concurrent singles by one artist on the Hot 100 was nine (by Elvis Presley, 19th December 1956).

The Beatles are the only artists to have 'back-to-back-to-back' number one singles on Billboard's Hot 100. Boyz II Men and Elvis Presley have succeeded themselves on the chart, but The Beatles are the only artist to 'three-peat.'

Sir Joseph Lockwood, chairman of EMI, presents the Beatles with two silver discs, to mark the 1/4 million plus sales of their two long playing records, Please, Please Me and With The Beatles, November 18th, 1963

AILY ECHO
TRIUMPH FOR BEATLES
SHOW BIZ WELCOME
EXTRA
THE BEATLES
BEATAX
BEATLES TO APPEAR ON GRANADA

THE BEATLES: EXTRAORDINARY FACTS AND FIGURES

'The Beatles' Yesterday is the most covered song in history, appearing in the Guinness Book of Records with over three thousand recorded versions.

'The Beatles even had their own stamp commissioned; featuring a tribute to Yellow Submarine.

'The Beatles had the fastest selling single of all time with I Want To Hold Your Hand. The song sold 250,000 units within three days in the U.S., one million in 2 weeks. (Additionally, it sold 10,000 copies per hour in New York City alone for the first 20 days.)

'The Beatles have the fastest selling CD of all time with 1. It sold over 13 million copies in four weeks.

'The largest number of advance orders for a single, at 2.1 million copies in the U.S. for Can't Buy Me Love (it sold 940,225 copies on its first day of release in the U.S. alone).

The cover of the single Yesterday

The Beatles perform I Want To Hold Your Hand on Granada TV's Late Scene Extra on November 25th, 1963

269

The Beatles perform in a
record shop to promote
the release of their album
Please Please Me on
March 22nd, 1963

THE BEATLES: EXTRAORDINARY FACTS AND FIGURES

Sgt. Pepper's Lonely Hearts Club Band is the best selling album of all time in the UK (over 4.5 million copies sold).

With their performance at Shea Stadium in 1965, The Beatles set new world records for concert attendance (55,600+) and revenue.

The Beatles broke television ratings records in the U.S. with their first appearance on The Ed Sullivan Show.

On June 30th 1966, The Beatles became the first musical group to perform at the Nippon Budokan Hall in Tokyo. They performed five times in three days gathering audiences of about 10,000 per performance.

Lennon (right) and McCartney at the Granville Studio performing on 'Shindig' in 1964

The Beatles, performing on the Ed Sullivan Show, New York City, February 9th, 1964

The Beatles rehearse on stage at the Deauville Hotel
for a performance on the Ed Sullivan Show

Incorporating pop art on their album covers, and introducing beatnik and psychedelic filmmaking to the masses, they explored every territory and every medium they had available.

And, most importantly, they took inspiration and change from the creative minds and spirits they met during their career. After meeting Dylan, they used cannabis to explore new thinking and songwriting, to take their musical connection to a deeper level.

After exploring Eastern philosophy, they learned new instruments and ways to view life, through meditation.

Despite this existentialist, experimental approach that helped evolve The Beatles, most of The Beatles most popular and well-known songs are the ones that fans enjoy singing along to. Love songs like Hey Jude and Something capture the feelings and experiences of life that the majority of people relate to. They were incredible at delivering the messages of life, love, and the world around us.

Much of that, of course, was because of the magical Lennon-McCartney songwriting partnership. But it was also because of the unique and carefully cultivated talents of each member of the group.

Whether it's in the bass line, the sound of the sitar, or the note of the keyboard, The Beatles managed to reach people with their music.

Culturally, The Beatles made waves.

Paul McCartney meditating in 1967

The cover of the 45rpm single Hey Jude, which features an image of an apple on the label, 1968

George Harrison with Ravi Shankar in 1967, who introduced him to Eastern instruments, like the sitar, and to World Music ways of playing

*The Beatles on stage
during a concert in the
United States, 1964*

Workmen and schoolchildren mob the car carrying British pop sensation The Beatles from Adelaide airport during their Australian tour, 1964

In January of 1964, Life magazine claimed, "A Beatle who ventures out unguarded into the streets runs the very real peril of being dismembered or crushed to death by his fans."

Girls arguably led this teenage obsession. As the 60s brought change and awareness of new possibilities, The Beatles managed to speak to a generation of young women on a new level. It was mostly about sex.

Why else would teenage girls behave in such strange ways? Greeting the band in mobs of hundreds, then thousands, hysterical, crying, fainting, and exhausting themselves, the young women who were fans of The Beatles were suddenly carefree from legal and social behavior that was expected of them.

When The Beatles played the London Palladium in October of 1963, riots broke out between teenage girls and police officers. It reportedly lasted four hours and left nine in hospital.

One explanation for the frenzy, the sexual revolution, is supported by the fact that unlike acts before them, The Beatles told the media and their fans exactly what they thought. They talked openly about themselves, with a sense of humor, and expressed their opinions through their music, their lyrics, and their comments to the media.

Young Beatles fans let loose with shrieks during concert at Shea Stadium, 1965

*Promotional portrait of the British
rock band The Beatles, circa 1963*

Ringo Starr on a beach in Miami, Florida, getting kissed by female fans, February 1964

They also challenged the status quo for male attractiveness. They were androgynous, almost normal or average looking and yet they were sexy. They went out with glamorous women, married models and actresses.

And they displayed a blatant disregard for authority. The Beatles arguably gave young women and men permission to be different, to question the rules and the law. For the first time, someone in the spotlight was asking, 'Is this right?' and 'Should it be different?'

Interestingly, this is supported by Sociologist and activist Barabara Ehrenreich, whose research demonstrated that on their debut, the typical crazed fan of The Beatles was predominately female, white, from a middle-class background, and on average 10 to 14 years.

One fan, Elizabeth Hess, accounted her experiences in an article in the Village Voice in 1994, "My own consciousness snapped into shape in 1964 at a Beatles concert. I still remember melting into a massive crowd of jumping, screaming girls, all thinking and feeling the same lascivious thoughts. It was my generation's turn to let our libidos go public. I was 12, just beginning to understand that sex was power: my first feminist epiphany. As the '60s tore on, the crowd of girls, now women, was still moving together, marching against the war in Vietnam."

While the debate over The Beatles legacy in a social and cultural sense continues, healthily, the black and white evidence of their legacy in the music world is obvious.

The first group to reject the writers usually afforded pop and rock acts, they wrote their own material and were the first to use the recording studio as a writing tool.

Using new and sometimes complex techniques, they built up song arrangements using multi-tracking and orchestral arrangements, as well as never-tried-before effects. And they did so including their love of folk rock, blues, country, jazz, and other genres.

"Honestly, if I hadn't seen them with my own eyes I'd have thought they were a colored group from back home."

– *Little Richard*

The Beatles enjoying the
Florida sunshine in 1964

Promotional portrait of the British
rock band The Beatles, circa 1963

Lennon gives it his all on tour in America, 1965

This is where their influence over future artists like Elton John, Pink Floyd, and even Nirvana started.

Dave Grohl loves The Beatles. The former drummer for 90s band Nirvana, who were the poster-band for the grunge movement, has spoken of his appreciation for The Beatles. Inspired by Starr, Grohl also talked of the influence the band had on lead singer Kurt Cobain. "Kurt loved The Beatles because it was just so simple."

In his new musical life as the lead singer and founder of the rock group The Foo Fighters, Grohl wrote a note to accompany a new release of Tomorrow Never Knows, "If it weren't for The Beatles, I would not be a musician. From a very young age I became fascinated with their songs, and over the years have drowned myself in the depth of their catalogue. Their groove and their swagger. Their grace and their beauty. Their dark and their light. The Beatles seemed to be capable of anything."

McCartney turns up his bass on set at Teddington Studios, 1964

In the late 1980s, a new group surfaced from Manchester, sporting Beatle-esque hairstyles. The Stone Roses hit the charts with guitar-style and song arrangements that were inspired by The Beatles and guitarist John Squire acknowledged them as one of his main influences.

Later, in the 90s, another group from Manchester took almost direct inspiration from The Beatles: Oasis.

"It's beyond an obsession. It's an ideal for living. I don't even know how to justify it to myself. With every song that I write, I compare it to The Beatles," Noel Gallagher said in an interview with Q magazine in 1996.

Oasis' debut album, Definitely Maybe, whispered The Beatles, in their melodies and arrangements. And they were unashamed to say that their success was based on their own rocked up, controversial style influenced by The Beatles.

Oasis' frontman, Liam Gallagher, even named his first son, Lennon.

"I love The Beatles. I haven't named any kids after them but I still really love them. They were the first group that I was ever properly aware of. In my early teens I would sometimes stay in and listen to the radio all day in the hope that I would catch a song by them that I'd never heard before and be able to tape it on my radio-cassette player."

– Jarvis Cocker

Liam and Noel Gallagher of Oasis

Ian Brown and his fellow Stone Roses
modeled their look on The Beatles

The Verve based songs from their first album
on melodies made famous by The Beatles

MUSICIANS INSPIRED BY THE FAB FOUR TODAY

Radiohead credited The Beatles as their key influence in 1997's OK Computer and 2003's Hail To The Thief.

Electric Light Orchestra declared their Beatles influence from the start, they wanted to continue where I Am Walrus left off.

Tori Amos claimed that her love of The Beatles was why she embraced rock and often covers the band's songs in her live shows.

Green Day's tracks Last Night On Earth and Viva La Gloria are said to feature Fab Four rhythms.

The Verve's album Bitter Sweet Symphony was said to have been influenced by The Beatles.

Franz Ferdinand said of The Beatles, "We always loved that, for example you'd hear The Beatles anthology discs and you'd hear them doing the demos and it's nice to hear that the best songwriters in the world started off and they couldn't get the song together in the beginning."

Other artists who count The Beatles as their main or one of their main influences include Jimi Hendrix, who covered some of their songs, Joe Cocker, David Bowie, and Keith Moon.

The Beatles legacy continues today, where the band's value is apparent through collectors' items that are bought and sold. In the US, a signed copy of the Sgt. Pepper's Lonely Hearts Club Band was bought at auction for $290,500 (£191,000) in 2013.

The previous record for an autographed Beatles album cover was $150,000 (£98,600) in 2011, for the 1964 record, Meet The Beatles.

Radiohead's albums were heavily influenced by the sound of The Beatles

"Our influences are who we are. It's rare that anything is an absolutely pure vision; even Daniel Johnston sounds like The Beatles. And that's the problem with the bands I'm always asked about, the ones derivative of the early Seattle sound. They don't dilute their influences enough."

– Eddie Vedder

"I just got into The Beatles a couple years ago, you know, I like it."

– Ziggy Marley

"I grew up in the day when The Beatles sold 1 million singles in a week. And all you've got to do now is sell about 10,000 singles and you're in the charts."

– Phil Collins

"I don't think anybody comes close to The Beatles, including Oasis."

– Brian May

Phil Collins lavishes the highest praise upon The Beatles

Ziggy Marley, a true Beatles fan

*Brian May often speaks of the Beatles
far-reaching and on-going influence
over modern popular music*

"My favorite artists have always been Elvis and The Beatles and they still are!"

– *Johnny Ramone*

"You know, I was such a big Beatles fan, and when I'd buy a new album I'd invariably hate it the first time I heard it 'cause it was a mixture of absolute joy and absolute frustration. I couldn't grasp what they'd done, and I'd hate myself for that."

– *Andy Partridge of XTC*

"We were driving through Colorado, we had the radio on, and eight of the Top 10 songs were Beatles songs... I Wanna Hold Your Hand, all those early ones. They were doing things nobody was doing. Their chords were outrageous, just outrageous, and their harmonies made it all valid... I knew they were pointing the direction of where music had to go."

– *Bob Dylan*

The Beatles (top to bottom) Paul McCartney, John Lennon, George Harrison, and Ringo Starr backstage at the London Palladium, 1963

The Beatles wearing blazers and boaters on the Night of a Hundred Stars show

"There was always a lot of American music in England until, obviously when The Beatles came around, then there was a shift towards English music, but before then American music was the main thing."

– *John Deacon of Queen*

"You can't be greater than Elvis, change things as much as The Beatles, or be as original as Led Zeppelin. All you can do is rip them off."

– *Billy Corgan*

"The Beatles were the band that made me realize it was possible to make a living as a musician, … When I heard The Beatles, I said, 'That's what I want to do!'"

– *Billy Joel*

The Beatles arrive at London Airport February 6th, 1964, after a trip to Paris in 1964

"The Beatles saved the world from boredom."

– *George Harrison*

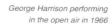

George Harrison performing in the open air in 1966

An iconic group shot used for the Twist & Shout EP, 1963

Index

The Beatles pose in the sea at Miami Beach during the band's tour of America